Harmony Singing

A Guide to Creative Harmony and Arranging

Alfred, the leader in educational publishing, and the National Guitar Workshop, one of America's finest guitar schools, have joined forces to bring you the best, most progressive educational tools possible. We hope you will enjoy this book and encourage you to look for other fine products from Alfred and the National Guitar Workshop.

ISBN 0-7390-2811-1 (Book and CD)

This book was acquired, edited and produced by Workshop Arts, Inc., the publishing arm of the National Guitar Workshop.
Nathaniel Gunod, acquisitions and editor
Michael Rodman, editor
Matt Cramer, music typesetter
Tim Phelps, interior design
CD recorded at Bar None Studios, Northford, CT

Microphone photo: courtesy of Shure Incorporated

SUSAN MAZER

TABLE OF CONTENTS

00

A compact disc is included with this book. This disc will make learning with the book easier and more enjoyable. The symbol shown at the left appears next to every example that is on the CD. Use the CD to help ensure that you're capturing the feel of the examples, interpreting the rhythms correctly, and so on. The track number below the symbol corresponds directly to the example you want to hear. Track 1 is a spoken introduction to the CD.

ABOUT THE AUTHOR

Philadelphia-born Susan Mazer lives and works in Connecticut. She received her Bachelor of Music degree from the Hartt School of Music. A faculty member at The Hartford Conservatory, she has also taught fingerstyle guitar at the National Guitar Workshop since 1989. Susan has been performing for 15 years with an acoustic duo and is the author of the popular instructional books *Guitar for the Absolute Beginner*, Books 1 and 2, and *Learn to Sing and Play Guitar*, all published by the National Guitar Workshop/Alfred.

DEDICATION

Thank you to my mother Judy for being everything to me. I appreciate all the things you've done for me in the past and the love and support you continue to give.

ACKNOWLEDGMENTS

Thank you to all of my students who teach me so much, Nat Gunod, Michael Rodman, Matthew Cramer, Sara Smolen, Joseph Demarest, Luke Scott, the Smolovers, the Workshop gang, Alison, Jackie Jarrett, Jerry Schurr, Carol, Jean, my parents, Mindy and most of all to Joe, who gives me something other than music to love.

INTRODUCTION

The human voice is one of the most beautiful sounds there is. Combining the textures, ranges and other qualities of different voices is an art. As in any art, there are no absolute rights or wrongs. There are, however, some basic tools and guidelines that will help you create a successful vocal arrangement.

We're all born with a natural ability to sing. Many accomplished vocalists may have no formal training, while others may have years of study and performing experience to their credit. Regardless of your past experience, there is always more to learn. Knowledge is power! The more you know about the voice and about the elements of a good arrangement, the better you'll be able to create your own arrangements and add new flavor to your repertoire. As you learn new techniques and concepts, you'll find creative ways to apply them to your own singing.

Though several topics are reviewed, this book assumes you have some prior experience as a singer and that you have some understanding of music notation and music theory, including time signatures, rhythms, note values, intervals, chords and chord types (including 7th chords), chord functions and basic chord progressions. (A good resource for understanding and reviewing these and other topics is *Essentials of Music Theory: Complete*, published by Alfred.)

Harmony Singing begins with the basics of music, including reading and essential theory. With these tools, you'll be able to understand the inner workings of the melodies and the two-, three- and four-part arrangements that come later in the book. You'll find an overview of the history of vocal music from Renaissance to rock, as well as a section that compares the styles of famous twentieth-century and modern vocal groups. By the end of the book, you'll have the chance to use the tools and skills you've developed to create and sing your own vocal harmonies.

One definition of harmony is the combination of tones that, when played or sung together, are pleasing to the ear. The most important piece of advice I'll give you before we begin is to use your ears. Try singing along with everything you hear. It may be a matter of trial and error, but in the end, you're the judge of what sounds good. At the same time, don't forget to use your head. If the perfect harmony doesn't present itself right away, use the skills you learn in this book to help you make good choices. Since harmony singing by definition involves more than one voice, see if you can find a partner to help you practice what you learn. When I was young, my mother would sit on the edge of my bed and sing harmonies with me. By the time I had outgrown being put to bed, I had the skills to sing along with anything.

Good luck!

Spem in Alium, a choral work by British composer Thomas Tallis (around 1505–1585), has parts for 40 different voices.

While still a high-school student, Mary Travers (of Peter, Paul and Mary) sang in a chorus that backed up folk legend Pete Seeger on his Folkways recordings.

CHAPTER 1
GETTING STARTED

HELPFUL TOOLS

Here are some of the tools that you'll find helpful to have on hand as you make your way through this book:

1. **Staff paper**. Use horizontal-format (or "landscape") manuscript paper. The extra width gives you more room to see the separate parts, and since there are fewer line of music per page, there's plenty of room to write in lyrics.

2. **Pencils and erasers**. We all make mistakes, so use these instead of ink pens and keep plenty on hand. As you become more proficient, you may want to invest in music notation software for your computer. Programs such as Finale® (Coda Music Technology) have special features that greatly streamline the process as you make vocal and choral arrangements.

3. **A piano or other instrument that will allow you to play chords**. For many arrangers, a piano is their most valuable tool. If you don't own a piano, an electronic keyboard or synthesizer will do just as well. Those that allow you to record and store separate tracks are especially useful for arranging.

4. **A recording device**. Your ears have the final word when it comes to judging the effectiveness of vocal harmonies. A great way to practice is to record yourself singing one part, and then to sing the other part over the playback. While it's something you don't really need as a beginner, a multitrack recorder, which allows you to record and individually control multiple vocal parts, can be a helpful tool for more advanced arrangers. When you become advanced enough to need one of these, you'll know it!

5. **A listening list**. Listening to music by different artists in different styles can be one of the most effective ways to stimulate your imagination. Keep an open mind and don't be afraid to listen to things you haven't heard before; even if they're not to your liking, you may pick up some useful tips, tricks and techniques.

6. **A friend to sing with**. Singing along with a recording isn't nearly as fun as singing along with a real person, and a tape recorder certainly can't match the subtlety and give-and-take of a performance with another singer. As you learn the arrangements in this book and create your own, try them out with a partner. You'll be surprised how much this adds to the learning experience.

Early in their careers, pop icons Simon and Garfunkel billed themselves as Tom and Jerry.

Songwriter Irving Berlin is said to have preferred Fred Astaire's renditions of his songs to those of any other performer.

HOW THE VOICE WORKS

The vibration of the *vocal cords* is what produces the sound of your voice. The vocal cords are a set of rubber band–like muscular folds. Air pushes through them, and like the reed of a wind instrument, they vibrate and produce sound. The different pitches a voice produces are the combined result of the tension, length and mass of the cords. The quality and range of each voice are different according to the differences among these factors.

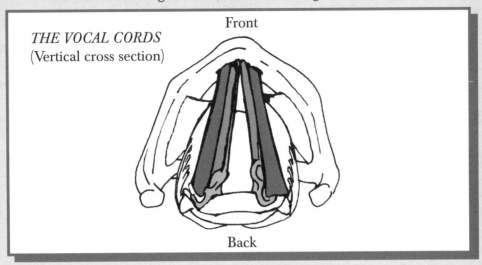

Front

THE VOCAL CORDS
(Vertical cross section)

Back

The vocal cords are attached to the *larynx*, also known as the *voice box*. The larynx, located at the top of your windpipe and made up of cartilage and muscle, is a key element in producing good vocal vibration and tone. The larynx is only partly responsible for the volume and musical qualities of your voice When you sing, in fact, your whole body works as a sounding board and an amplifier.

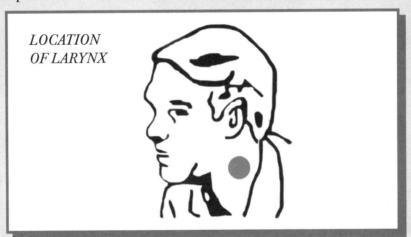

LOCATION OF LARYNX

The main *resonators* (amplifying chambers) used in singing are the throat, the mouth, the nose and the sinus cavities, which are illustrated on the next page. As you sing, the throat should remain free and open. Proper singing posture, which includes keeping your back straight and your shoulders level, helps insure that the neck and body are aligned so that you can use your throat effectively and to best advantage.

GOOD SINGING POSTURE

From the throat, the sound travels to the mouth. The positions of your jaw, tongue, lips and *palate* (roof of the mouth) all affect the sound you produce. Keeping the mouth loose and open as you sing will result in a clearer, louder tone.

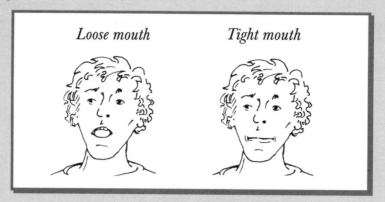

Loose mouth   *Tight mouth*

Though you may not realize it, the nose is also a resonator; think of the way your voice changes when you pinch off your nose. The sinuses also play an important part in resonance; they should tingle with vibration when you sing. In order to find proper placement for the voice, many teachers will have you visualize the sound in the sinus area.

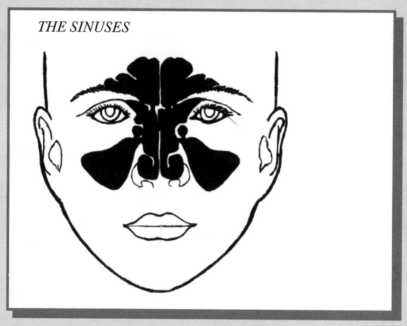

THE SINUSES

Breathing from the *diaphragm* is key to a strong, full singing voice. The diaphragm is a U-shaped partition of muscle and connective tissue between the chest cavity and abdominal cavity. As you inhale, the diaphragm lowers; as you exhale, the diaphragm raises, pushing up the lungs. If you are breathing properly, the area around your waist and back should expand as you inhale without causing your chest to rise or your shoulders to shrug. Breathing in this way allows you to take fuller breaths, enabling you to sing longer and stronger.

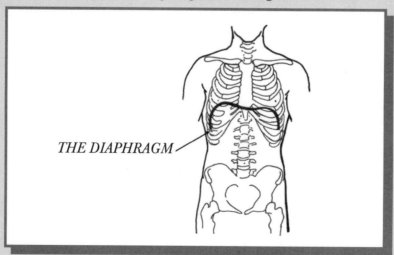

THE DIAPHRAGM

CHAPTER 2
MUSIC THEORY FOR VOCALISTS

PITCH

A *pitch* is the specific degree of highness or lowness of a musical sound. Pitches take their names from the first seven letters of the alphabet: A, B, C, D, E, F and G. Once you reach G, the pattern begins again: A B C D E F G A B C D E F G A, and so on.

NOTES

A *note* is a symbol that stands for a musical sound:

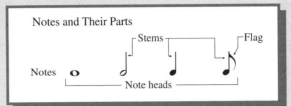

STAVES

Specific pitches are indicated by their placement of notes on a *staff* (plural: *staves*). A staff is made up of five horizontal lines with four spaces in between. Each line and space represents a pitch. Notes are written either directly on these lines or in the spaces.

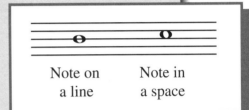

CLEFS

Every staff begins with a *clef*, which is a symbol that tells you the name of each line and space. The *treble clef* is also called the *G clef*, because it loops around the G line on its staff. Notice that notes too high or low to be written on the staff are written with *ledger lines*. *Middle C* is the C that corresponds to the C approximately in the center of the piano keyboard.

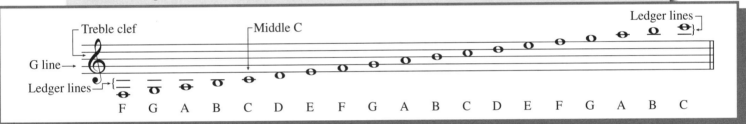

The *bass clef* is also called the *F clef*, because its hook and two dots show you the F line on its staff.

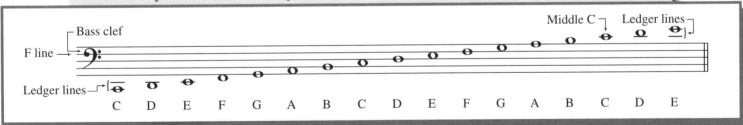

TIME

MEASURES AND BAR LINES

The staff is divided by vertical lines called *bar lines*. The space between two bar lines is called a *measure*. Measures divide music into groups of *beats*. A beat is an equal division of time. Beats are the basic pulse behind music. A *double bar* marks the end of a section or example.

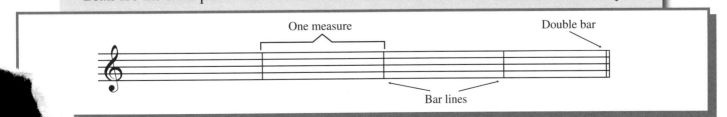

NOTE AND REST VALUES

As you know, the location of a note relative to the staff tells us the pitch of the note. The duration, or *value*, is indicated by the appearance of the note. Here are the note values (assume a quarter note equals one beat) and their corresponding *rests*, which indicate a measured silence. A whole rest is used to fill up the musical space in an empty measure, no matter what the time signature is.

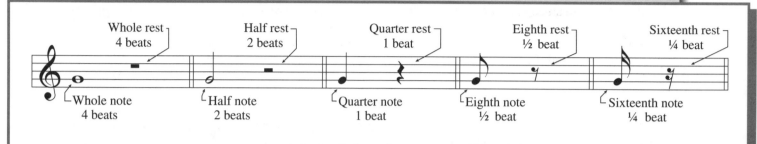

This chart shows the relationships among the note values. Keep in mind that these note values have corresponding rest values.

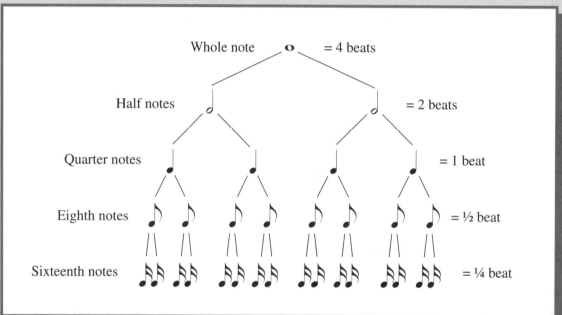

TIME SIGNATURES

Every piece of music has numbers at the beginning that tell us how to count the time.

The top number represents the number of beats, or counts, per measure.

The bottom number represents the type of note receiving one beat.

$\frac{4}{4}$ 4 beats per measure
Quarter note ♩ = one beat

$\frac{3}{4}$ 3 beats per measure
Quarter note ♩ = one beat

$\frac{6}{8}$ 6 beats per measure
Eighth note ♪ = one beat

Sometimes a **C** is used in place of $\frac{4}{4}$, which is also called *common time*.

BEAMING

Notes that are less than one beat in duration are often beamed together. Notice the counting numbers: Since there are four sixteenth notes in a beat, they are counted "1 e & a 2 e & a," etc.

TIES

When notes with the same pitch are *tied*, the second note isn't sung or played again. Rather, its value is added to that of the first note. So, a half note tied to a quarter note equals three beats.

Notice the numbers under the staff in the following examples. They indicate how to count. Both of these examples are in $\frac{4}{4}$ time, so we count four beats in each measure. When there are eighth notes, which are only half a beat, we count "&" ("and") to show the division of the beat into two parts. When a counting number is in parentheses, a note is held with a tie rather than rearticulated.

Using ties is a convenient way to notate notes that begin off the beat (on an "&").

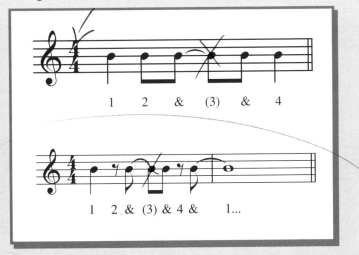

DOTS

A dot increases the length of a note by half its original value. For instance, a half note equals two beats, and half its value is one beat (a quarter note), so a *dotted half note* equals three beats (2 + 1 = 3). Another way to think of it is that a dotted half note is equal to a half note tied to a quarter note.

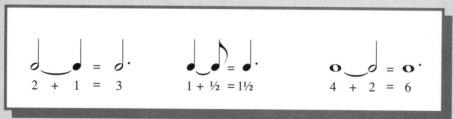

Dotted notes are especially important when the time signature is $\frac{3}{4}$, because the longest note that will fit into a measure is a dotted half note. Dotted notes are also very important in $\frac{6}{8}$ time, because not only is a dotted half note the longest possible note, but a dotted quarter note equals exactly half a measure (counted 1 & a 2 & a).

TRIPLETS

A triplet is a group of three notes that divides a beat (or beats) into three equal parts.

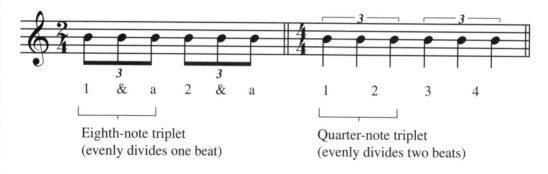

REPEAT SIGNS

These signs are used to indicate that music should be repeated.

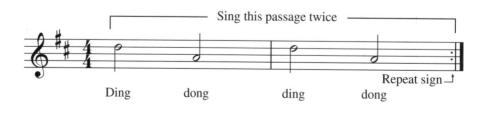

WHOLE STEPS AND HALF STEPS

The keyboard provides a helpful visual refernce when discussing certain pitch relationships. On a keyboard, the white keys are arranged in alphabetical order. As a point of reference, C is always the white key to the immediate left of a pair of black keys.

The closest distance between any two notes on the keyboard is a *half step*. For example, the distance from a black key to the white key on either side of it is a half step. Two half steps make up a *whole step*. For example, two white keys with a black key between them are a whole step apart.

W = Whole step

H = Half step

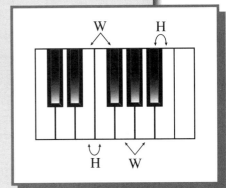

ACCIDENTALS

Signs called *accidentals* change the pitch of a note. A *flat* (♭) lowers the pitch of a note by a half step. For example, D♭ is the black key just to the left of the D key.

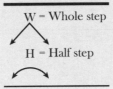

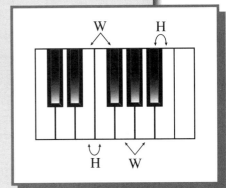

A *sharp* (♯) raises the pitch of a note by a half step. For example, C♯ is the black key just to the right of the C key.

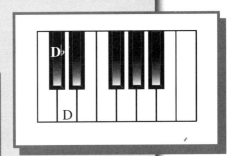

Both flats and sharps apply only to the exact line or space in the measure in which they appear. Flats and sharps can be cancelled with a *natural* (♮).

Every flat note can be called by a sharp name, and every sharp note can be called by a flat name. They look different in written music, but they sound the same. Notes that sound the same but have different names are called *enharmonic* notes.

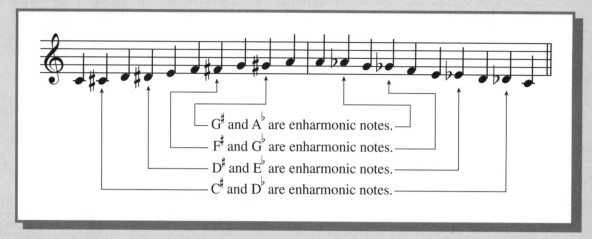

G♯ and A♭ are enharmonic notes.
F♯ and G♭ are enharmonic notes.
D♯ and E♭ are enharmonic notes.
C♯ and D♭ are enharmonic notes.

THE MAJOR SCALE

A *scale* is a group of notes arranged in a specific order of half steps and whole steps. One of the most commonly used scales is the *major scale.* The pattern of whole and half steps that makes up a major scale is often called the *major scale formula,* shown in the chart below:

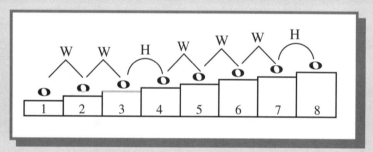

*NSYNC members J. C. Chasez and Justin Timberlake were regulars on the Disney Channel's Mickey Mouse Club before forming one of the most popular vocal groups of the 1990s.

The Chiffons' publishers successfully sued George Harrison for copyright infringement, claiming that the ex-Beatle's hit "My Sweet Lord" bore more than a passing resemblance to their earlier chart-topper "He's So Fine."

A scale can start on any note. Each note in a scale is assigned a *degree* based on its position—the first note is the first degree, the second note is the second degree, and so on. The first degree of a scale, called the *tonic*, is the note that gives the scale its name. A major scale that begins on C, for example, is called the C Major scale. C Major is the only major scale that has no sharps or flats. Every other major scale uses a different number of sharps or flats (never both) in order to make the pattern of whole and half steps fit the major scale formula. For example, the G Major scale has one sharp note, F♯. The F Major scale has one flat note, B♭. Since they're both major scales, the pattern of half steps and whole steps is the same.

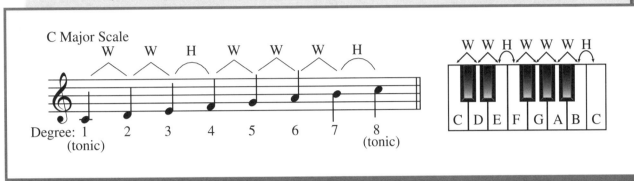

A special set of syllables called *solfège syllables* can be useful when you sing major scales that begin on different notes. Each syllable stands for a different scale degree.

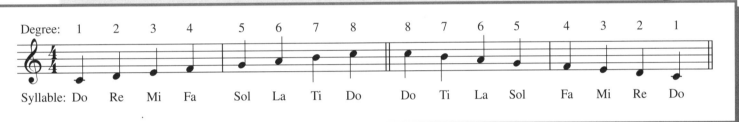

DEGREE		SYLLABLE
1	=	Do (*doh*)
2	=	Re (*ray*)
3	=	Mi (*mee*)
4	=	Fa (*fah*)
5	=	Sol (*sole*)
6	=	La (*lah*)
7	=	Ti (*tee*)
8	=	Do (*doh*)

The Dixie Chicks took their name from the Little Feat song "Dixie Chickens."

Pop sensation Ricky Martin began his musical career as a member of Menudo, a Puerto Rican vocal group that originally forced its members to "retire" at the age of 16.

Here are the major scales you'll encounter most often. Notice that even though each begins on a different note, all of the scales are constructed according to the major scale formula.

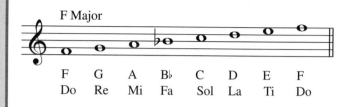

FLAT KEYS

F Major
F G A B♭ C D E F
Do Re Mi Fa Sol La Ti Do

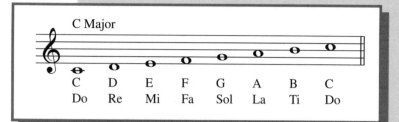

C Major
C D E F G A B C
Do Re Mi Fa Sol La Ti Do

SHARP KEYS

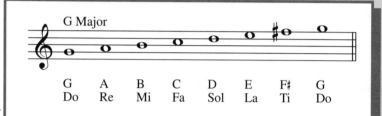

G Major
G A B C D E F♯ G
Do Re Mi Fa Sol La Ti Do

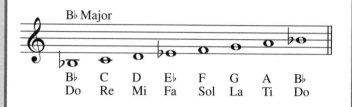

B♭ Major
B♭ C D E♭ F G A B♭
Do Re Mi Fa Sol La Ti Do

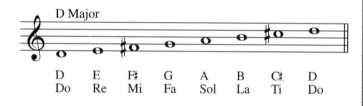

D Major
D E F♯ G A B C♯ D
Do Re Mi Fa Sol La Ti Do

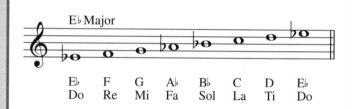

E♭ Major
E♭ F G A♭ B♭ C D E♭
Do Re Mi Fa Sol La Ti Do

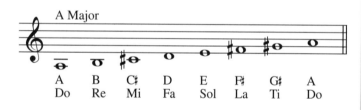

A Major
A B C♯ D E F♯ G♯ A
Do Re Mi Fa Sol La Ti Do

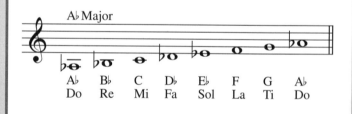

A♭ Major
A♭ B♭ C D♭ E♭ F G A♭
Do Re Mi Fa Sol La Ti Do

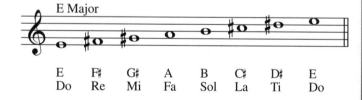

E Major
E F♯ G♯ A B C♯ D♯ E
Do Re Mi Fa Sol La Ti Do

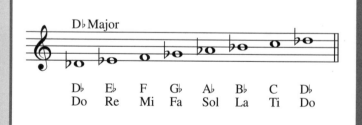

D♭ Major
D♭ E♭ F G♭ A♭ B♭ C D♭
Do Re Mi Fa Sol La Ti Do

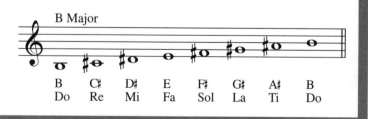

B Major
B C♯ D♯ E F♯ G♯ A♯ B
Do Re Mi Fa Sol La Ti Do

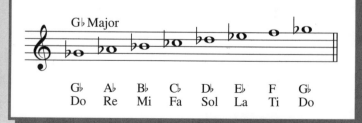

G♭ Major
G♭ A♭ B♭ C♭ D♭ E♭ F G♭
Do Re Mi Fa Sol La Ti Do

12/4/18

KEYS AND KEY SIGNATURES

Most pieces are based on a particular scale and uses mainly notes from that scale. One note of that scale, the tonic, is usually more important than the others. This note is often the note on which a melody begins or ends, and it serves as a kind of "home base," or *tonal center*. This tonal center is often referred to as the *key*. For example, if a piece uses mainly notes from the C Major scale, and C is the tonal center, we say that the piece is in the key of C Major. As is true of scales, the note that gives a key its name is called the *tonic*.

You've already learned that in order to follow the correct pattern of whole steps and half steps in building a major scale, it's necessary to add either sharps or flats. For example, if you start a major scale on G, you always need one sharp (F♯). The sharps or flats you need to make a particular key are shown at the beginning of every staff, just to the right of the clef. This is called a *key signature*.

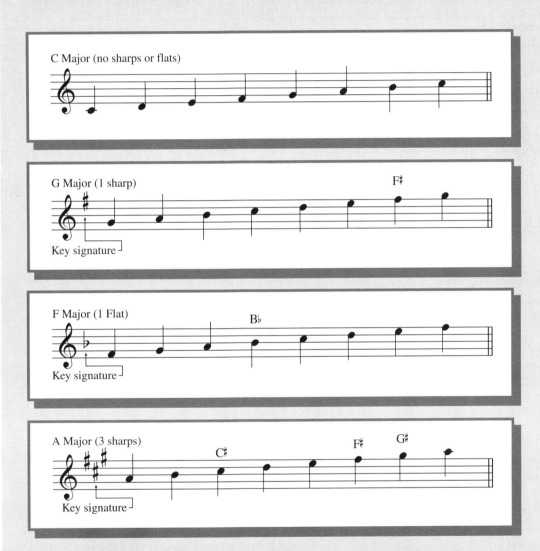

Notice that when there is a key signature, accidentals are not needed in front of the sharped or flatted notes. Instead, the sharps and flats in the key signature apply to the entire piece, and to every line and space with the same name, unless they're cancelled out by a natural sign.

The order of sharps or flats in a key signature is always the same. When sharps appear in a key signature, they always appear in this order:

This means that if a key signature has two sharps, they will always be F♯ and C♯; if it has three sharps, they will always be F♯, C♯ and G♯; and so on. You can use this phrase to help you remember the order of sharps in the key signature:

Fat Cows Go Down And Eat Breakfast

When flats appear in a key signature, they always appear in this order:

This means that if a key signature has two flats, they will always be B♭ and E♭; if it has three flats, they will always be B♭, E♭ and A♭; and so on. You can use this phrase to help you remember the order of flats in the key signature:

Be Ever Alert During Guitar Class, Friend

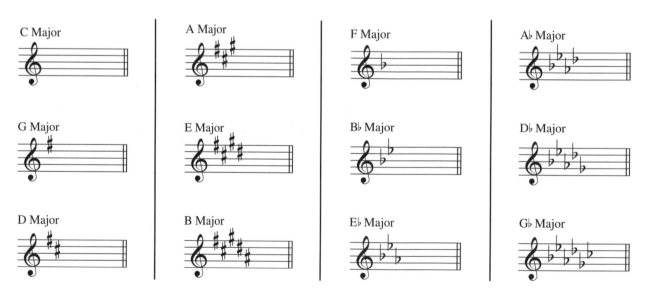

MAJOR KEY SIGNATURES

INTERVALS

PERFECT AND MAJOR INTERVALS

The specific distance between two notes is called an *interval*. Let's look at the intervals in a major scale (C Major), measuring from the root. Each of these intervals has either a *major* or *perfect* quality. By numbering the notes in the scale from 1 to 8, it's easy to learn the intervals. Counting up to each note from the root will give you the number name of the interval. Intervals can be either *harmonic* (notes sounding together) or *melodic* (notes sounding one at a time), but the name of the interval is the same in both cases. The intervals on this page are harmonic; we'll take a closer look at melodic intervals on page 20.

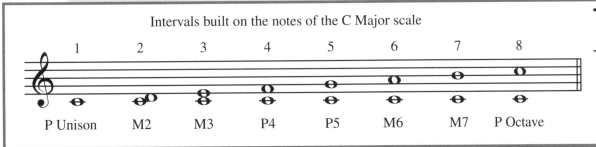

Intervals built on the notes of the C Major scale

P = Perfect
M = Major

1 2 3 4 5 6 7 8

P Unison   M2   M3   P4   P5   M6   M7   P Octave

MINOR INTERVALS

If you make a major interval smaller by a half step, it becomes a *minor* interval. You can make a major interval minor by lowering the top note with a flat (or a natural if the note is sharp).

m = minor

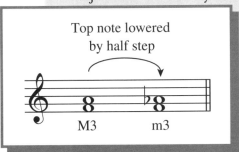

Top note lowered by half step

M3   m3

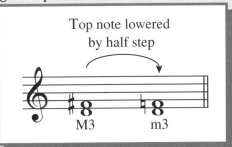

Top note lowered by half step

M3   m3

You can also make a major interval smaller by raising the bottom note by a half step. You can do this by raising the bottom note with a sharp (or a natural if the note is flat).

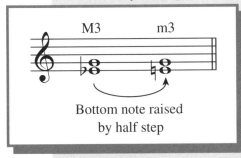

M3   m3

Bottom note raised by half step

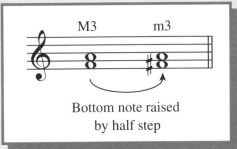

M3   m3

Bottom note raised by half step

AUGMENTED AND DIMINISHED INTERVALS

An interval a half step larger than a major or perfect interval is an *augmented* interval. 2nds, 4ths, and 6ths are the augmented intervals you'll encounter most often.

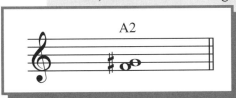

A2

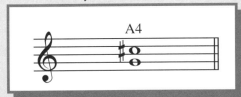

A4

A = Augmented
d = diminished

An interval a half step smaller than a minor interval is a *diminished interval*. 5ths and 7ths are the diminished intervals you'll encounter most often.

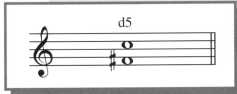

d5

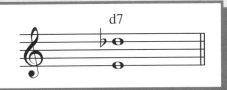

d7

IDENTIFYING INTERVALS BY SOUND

In making vocal arrangements, it's helpful to know what specific intervals sound like. Both melodic and harmonic intervals come into play—melodic intervals in a single vocal part, and harmonic intervals between different vocal parts. Every interval has a unique quality that contributes to the mood of an arrangement. One of the easiest ways to become familiar with the sound of different intervals is to think of how they're used in familiar tunes. For example, if you wanted to imagine what a major 2nd sounds like, you could think of the first two notes of "Frère Jacques" (sung on the word "frère"), which are a major 2nd apart. The chart below will give you some examples of tunes that can help you identify specific melodic intervals. (Unless otherwise specified, the interval in question is formed by the first two notes of the tune.) Try using these as a guideline for finding intervals in other tunes you know.

Unison	"Jingle Bells"
Minor 2nd	Theme from *Jaws*
Major 2nd	"Frère Jacques"
Minor 3rd	"What Child Is This?"
Major 3rd	"When the Saints Go Marching In"
Perfect 4th	"Here Comes the Bride"
Augmented 4th	"Maria" (from *West Side Story*)
Perfect 5th	"Twinkle, Twinkle, Little Star" (second and third notes)
Minor 6th	"Where Do I Begin?" (third and fourth notes; theme from *Love Story*)
Major 6th	"My Bonnie Lies Over the Ocean"
Minor 7th	Theme from *Star Trek* (original TV series)
Major 7th	"Bali Ha'i" (first and third notes; from *South Pacific*)
Perfect octave	"Over the Rainbow"

Notice the difference in quality between the different types of intervals. You'll soon learn how to use these intervals in creating beautiful arrangements.

CHAPTER 3
TIME TO SING

VOCAL RANGES

While each person's voice is unique, most voices fall into one of four main types defined by *range* (the entire compass, from low to high, of the pitches a singer can produce). Most female voices can be classified as either *soprano* (higher range) or *alto* (lower range), while most male voices are either *tenor* (higher range) or *bass* (lower range). While there are a number of intermediate ranges that overlap these four, vocal arrangements typically make use of some combination of soprano, alto, tenor and bass. As a unit, the soprano-alto-tenor-bass configuration (often abbreviated SATB) is very versatile and has been used for hundreds of years by composers and arrangers of vocal music.

Note in the illustrations below that each voice type is actually given two ranges. The *maximum range*, shown with black note heads, is an approximation of the very highest and lowest notes that can be sung by that voice type. Some singers can extend these ranges even further—upward, downward, or both—so the given maximum ranges are only typical. Because it's often difficult or uncomfortable for singers to sing at the very extremes of their ranges, the *practical range* for each voice type is shown with whole notes. The practical range may be regarded as the range that most singers of this type will find comfortable in most situations. The ranges you use when making arrangements will depend on a number of factors. As a rule of thumb, it's best to stick to practical ranges for singers who are young or inexperienced, or when you're unsure of the abilities of the singer(s) involved. It's also a good idea to use practical ranges for arrangements involving a large group, such as a choir, since not every singer in the group may have the ability or training to sing well at the extremes of his or her range.

Music for tenors is often written in the *tenor clef*, which looks like the treble clef with a small "8" under the curl. The "8" indicates that the music will actually sound an octave lower than written.

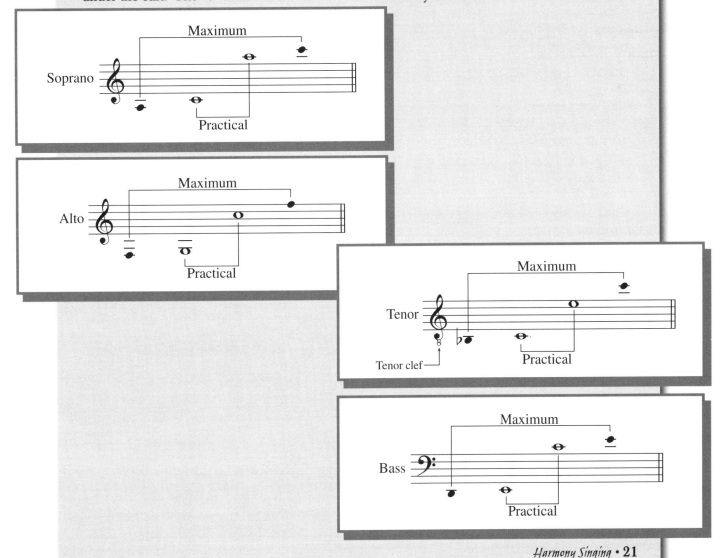

WARM-UPS

As with any type of exercise, warming up before you sing will help you avoid injury and use the muscles involved to best advantage. A 15–20 minute warm-up before singing will go a long way in helping you become a better singer. Each of the exercises on this page targets a different aspect of your voice. Since each exercise in this book is notated in only one way, singers should choose the octave that best suits his or her voice. For example, male singers will probably want to sing the exercises on this page an octave lower than written. By the same token, female singers who want to try examples or parts written in tenor or bass clefs should sing them in the appropriate higher octave.

BREATHING

When to breathe as you sing depends on both the music and the singer. The main idea to keep in mind as you breathe is that you want to take in enough air to support your voice and yet maintain a natural musical flow. As a rule of thumb, it's best to take breaths in places where they make the most sense and are least noticeable. For example, it makes less sense to take a breath in the middle of a phrase, where it interrupts the musical line, than it is to take a breath between phrases. In nearly all situations, taking full, quick, soundless breaths will give your voice the greatest amount of support.

Example 1 will help you develop breath control and focus your tone in your sinus cavities. Sing each of the examples on the given syllables, humming on "mmm." Continue the given pattern, moving up a half step at a time, stopping at the point where you feel a strain in your voice. Concentrate on producing a full, rich sound. The curved lines under the notes are called *slurs*. In vocal music, slurs are used to connect two or more different notes that are sung on the same syllable. Try taking a breath after each two-measure phrase. Use a piano or the CD for this book to find the correct pitch to sing.

Example 2 will help improve your pronunciation and tone. Since every voice has *breaks* (shifts in tone quality) that separate the low, medium and high ranges, warm-ups with larger skips are especially beneficial in focusing your sound.

Example 3 will help you increase your range. Notice that this example uses eighth-note triplets.

UNISONS AND DOUBLING

The most basic *texture* (number of parts) for multiple voices is the unison. In unison singing, all of the different vocalists' parts are identical (or an octave apart from one another). Unisons are especially effective in reinforcing melody lines.

Related to the unison is a technique called *doubling*. In doubling, a melody or other important line is reinforced at the unison or octave by at least one additional part, while one or more different parts provide harmony.

When Elvis Presley appeared on the Ed Sullivan Show in 1956, network censors directed that he be shown only from the waist up, lest his gyrating hips offend more sensitive viewers.

Peter, Paul and Mary's classic recording of "Puff the Magic Dragon" not only became a number-one single, but also made it to the R&B charts as a top-ten hit.

This arrangement of "Battle Hymn of the Republic" begins with the two highest parts in unison. In measure 9, the lowest voice adds a distinctly different line. Try singing along with this song on the CD. Begin by finding the part that best fits the range of your voice. Sing along with that part; once you've memorized it, try singing along (in a different octave if necessary) with both of the other parts. Notice that this song begins on a *pickup* (an incomplete measure at the beginning of a piece), in this case on the "and" of beat 4. The final, *incomplete measure* is shortened by the number of beats in the pickup, so that the total number of beats in the pickup and the incomplete measure is equal to one full measure.

BATTLE HYMN OF THE REPUBLIC

Julia Ward Howe
Traditional melody

The Kingston Trio got their start opening for comedian Phyllis Diller in a San Francisco nightclub.

With their 1981 album Mecca for Moderns, Manhattan Transfer became the first group in history to win Grammy Awards in the pop and jazz categories in the same year.

CHAPTER 4
TWO-PART HARMONY

CONSONANT AND DISSONANT INTERVALS

Traditional harmony comes with its own set of principles and guidelines, and one of the most important is that certain harmonic intervals work best in certain contexts. As we begin to look at two-part harmony, let's use as a working definition of harmony: "the combination of tones that when sounded together are pleasing to the ear." As you've probably recognized, certain harmonic intervals do sound more pleasing or "right" than others. Such intervals are often called *consonant* intervals. While consonance often depends on the context in which an interval is used, you can think of unisons, 3rds, 6ths, perfect 5ths and octaves as consonant intervals for our purposes. The "leftover" intervals—2nds, 4ths, 7ths and augmented or diminished intervals—are often described as *dissonant* intervals. Dissonant intervals are sometimes described as having a jarring or harsh quality. For voices in particular, careful control of consonance and dissonance is crucial to the success of an arrangement. We'll take a closer look at dissonant intervals on page 31.

Here's an exercise that will help you sing different intervals. Play or have someone sing middle C (male singers may want to use the C an octave lower). Then, try singing each interval in turn above this note. Listen for the unique quality and feeling of each interval. The number of half steps in each interval is given above the staff.

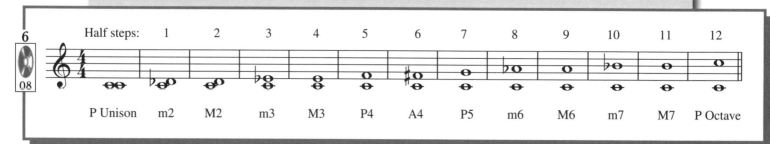

Because of their thin, exposed texture, two-part vocal arrangements are made up of mostly consonant intervals between the parts. In example 7, the bottom part (Voice 2) contains the melody, while the top part (Voice 1) provides the harmony. You can even think of the top part as a "shadow" of the main melody, since it closely follows the motion of the melody.

In this arrangement of "Sloop John B," the harmony part begins a 3rd above the melody, and the lines move mostly in 3rds throughout. Choose the part that best suits the range of the your voice. Sing along with that part on the CD until you've memorized it, and then try the other part.

SLOOP JOHN B

Traditional
Bahamian Song

MOTION OF TWO VOICES

So far, we've looked at the relationship between the voices in two-part harmony in terms of intervals—that is, how far apart the voices are from each other. Now, we'll take a look at how voices move in relation to one another. In example 7 on page 26, the motion of the harmony part in relation to the melody was described in terms of a shadow, since it closely followed the shape of the melody. This kind of motion, in which parts move in the same direction at the same time, is called *similar motion*.

The two parts of "Sloop John B" on page 27 not only move in similar motion, but the numeric interval between the parts (3rds) remains the same throughout most of the arrangement. Similar motion that maintains the same numeric interval is called *parallel motion*.

The opposite of similar motion is *contrary motion*. In contrary motion, parts move in opposite directions at the same time.

Motion in which one voice moves while the other remains stationary is called *oblique motion*.

It's worth noting that some of these types of motion work better with certain intervals than with others, and arrangements that use only one type of motion are fairly rare. Most often, you'll find these various motions used in different combinations within an arrangement. Mixing and matching will allow you great flexibility and help avoid monotony as you make your own arrangements for the voice. As always, your ears are the final judge as to what works best.

Examples 12–15 demonstrate the four types of motion explained on page 28. Notice that the top line in each case is the same. Practice these on the neutral syllable "la."

Since the two parts of example 15 use different rhythms, the syllables for the top part are given above the staff, while the syllables for the bottom part are in the usual position below the staff.

Some of the earliest vocal harmony consisted of two voices singing in parallel 4ths or 5ths.

Nominated 14 times over the course of his career, rock icon Elvis Presley won three Grammy Awards—all for gospel recordings.

COUNTERPOINT

One approach to two-part harmony is *counterpoint*. In simplest terms, counterpoint is the sounding of two or more different musical lines at the same time. In two-voice counterpoint, the melody is accompanied by an independent line called a *countermelody*. Instead of "shadowing" the melody as in example 7 on page 26, a true countermelody has a shape and character of its own. A countermelody can be either above or below the main melody.

PARTNER SONGS

Partner songs are pairs of songs that can be combined effectively in harmony because their harmonic structures are identical. Naturally, the *lyrics* (words) will be different, but singing partner songs can be a great way to develop your part-singing skills. Examples of partner songs include "When the Saints Go Marching In/Swing Low, Sweet Chariot" and "Battle Hymn of the Republic ('Glory, Glory Hallelujah' part)/Rocka My Soul."

The partner song on page 31 is made up of "He's Got the Whole World in His Hands" and "Rocka My Soul." Find a singing partner and choose your parts, or focus on one part as you listen to the CD. Once you've mastered your part, switch parts with your partner. If you used the CD, sing the part you didn't sing the first time. Notice that the top part begins with a pickup, and "Rocka My Soul" comes in on the first full measure.

"He's Got the Whole World in His Hands/Rocka My Soul" is performed with a long-short rhythmic pattern called *swing eighths* or *shuffle rhythm*. Swing eighths are written like even eighth notes but sound something like a triplet group in which the first two triplets are tied together.

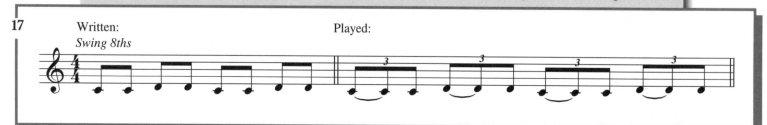

In this book, you'll find the phrase "Swing 8ths" at the beginning of examples that are to be sung with a swing feel.

This partner song also uses a number of dissonant intervals (or *dissonances*) between the voices. One thing to remember is that dissonances work best when they occur as the result of smooth, natural movement of individual lines, and when they *resolve* (move to a consonant interval, or *consonance*). In the second complete measure, for example, there is a dissonance of a major 2nd on the "and" of beat 3; Voice 2 sings D on the syllable "bra," while Voice 1 sings E on the syllable "He's." Notice that both notes are approached smoothly; the D in Voice 2 is the same note that was previously sung, and the E in Voice 1 is approached by step. After this point, the D in Voice 2 continues to move down by step, and on the next note (C♯) resolves the dissonance by creating a minor 3rd with Voice 1 (E). Look at the B♯s in Voice 2; sometimes they form consonances, and sometimes dissonances, against Voice 1, but in each case, they are approached and left in the same way (C♯–B♯–C♯). These B♯s, which are outside the main key (A Major), are called *chromatic tones*. Certain dissonances and chromatic tones, called *non-harmonic tones*, function in a very specific way that we'll take a look at beginning on page 39.

HE'S GOT THE WHOLE WORLD IN HIS HANDS/ROCKA MY SOUL

Traditional

CHAPTER 5
THREE-PART HARMONY

TRIADS

At this point, we've looked at both single-line melodies and two-part arrangements. Now, we'll look at the possibilities in using three voices at once, beginning with some helpful music theory.

A group of notes sounded together is called a *chord*. A chord made up of exactly three notes is called a *triad*. There are four main kinds of triads, each of which has a distinctive sound.

A triad built from the first, third and fifth notes (or degrees) of a major scale is called a *major triad*. When used in a triad, these notes are called the *root, 3rd* and *5th*. You can build a major triad by adding the notes a major 3rd and a perfect 5th above your chosen root, or by stacking a minor 3rd on top of a major 3rd. Major triads are sometimes described as having a bright or happy sound.

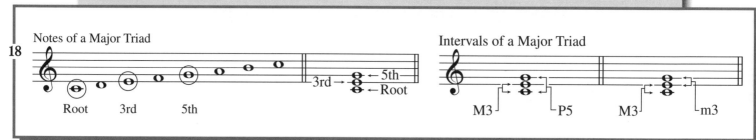

By lowering the 3rd of a major triad by a half step, you create a *minor triad*. This lowered 3rd is often shown as ♭3. You can build a minor triad by adding the notes a minor 3rd and perfect 5th above your chosen root, or by stacking a major 3rd on top of a minor 3rd. Minor triads are often described as having a dark or sad sound.

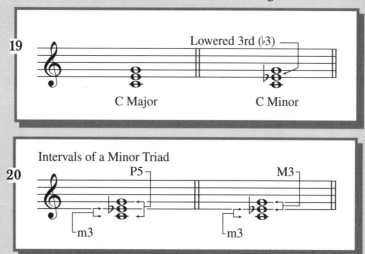

By lowering the 3rd and 5th of a major triad, you create a *diminished triad*. This lowered 5th is often shown as ♭5. You can also build a diminished triad by stacking one minor 3rd on top of another. Diminished triads are often described as having a tense or unstable sound.

_____

d = diminished

_____

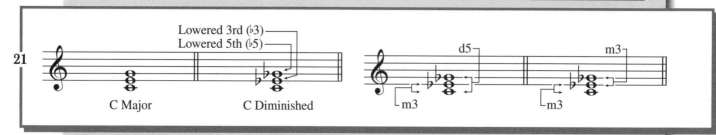

By raising the 5th (♯5) of a major triad by a half step, you create an *augmented triad*. You can also build an augmented triad by stacking one major 3rd on top of another. Though the feeling of an augmented triad is quite different from that of a diminished triad, it too is often described as having an unstable sound.

A = Augmented

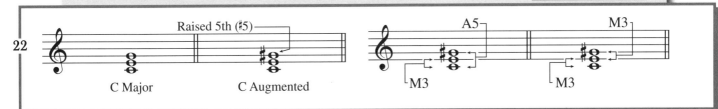

INVERSIONS

The notes of a triad won't always be arranged in the we've seen so far—that is, in *root position* (with the root as the bottom note). You can also rearrange the notes of the triad into *inversions,* which use a note other than the root as the bottom note. Two different inversions are possible for any triad.

Triads with the 3rd on the bottom are in *first inversion*.

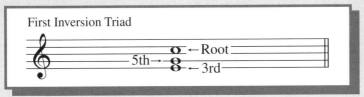

Triads with the 5th on the bottom are in *second inversion*.

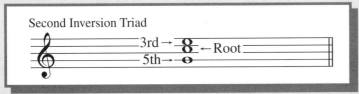

DIATONIC TRIADS

The triads built on each degree of the major scale, using only notes from the scale, are called *diatonic* triads. Triads are often labeled with uppercase or lowercase Roman numerals according to their quality (major, minor, etc.) and the scale degree they're built on. Notice that the vii chord, which is diminished, includes a small circle (∘) after the numeral.

ROMAN NUMERAL REVIEW

Uppercase = Major
Lowercase = minor or diminished

I or i.................1	IV or iv..........4	VII or vii.........7
II or ii.............2	V or v.............5	
III or iii..........3	VI or vi...........6	

Chord Symbols:
Major = Maj
minor = min
diminished = dim

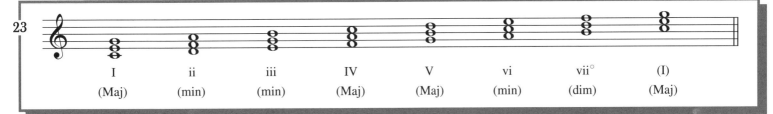

Try playing the diatonic triads on a piano or other instrument, beginning on different notes and applying the formulas you've learned for each. Singing each triad one note at a time, then see if you can find two other vocalists to sing the different triads with you, each of you taking a different note. Once you begin to make three-part arrangements, you'll find that this vocabulary of different triads will allow you to create a multitude of moods for the listener.

By now, you've probably realized that multiple voices create a fuller texture than a single voice, and that two-part harmony makes use of intervals that create a certain amount of tension and release through varying degrees of consonance and dissonance. Now, by adding a third voice, we have complete triads at our disposal.

Try this exercise in which three voices sing the triads built on every degree of the C Major scale. Try singing each part in turn, and use two other singers, a keyboard or other instrument, or the CD to fill in the rest of the texture. The solfège syllables are given for each note.

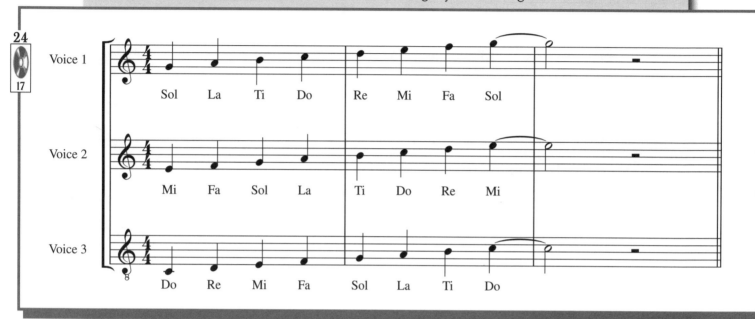

CHORD FUNCTIONS AND THE PRIMARY CHORDS

CHORD FUNCTIONS

On page 33, you learned about the diatonic triads. Knowing how the diatonic triads function and how to combine them in a way that makes musical sense is essential for creating good harmony parts and arrangements. Each diatonic triad has a Roman numeral name, but each one also has a *chord function* name.

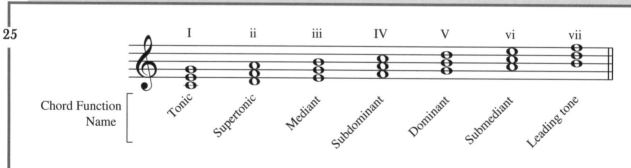

THE PRIMARY CHORDS

The three most important chords in any key are the tonic (I), subdominant (IV) and dominant (V).

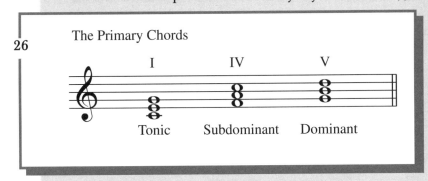

You may ask, "Why are these three chords so important?" That's a bit like asking, "Why is there air?" At least from where we sit in the twenty-first century, that's how it seems. In fact, the idea of primary chords was taught all the way back in the eighteenth century, in a theory book called *Treatise on Harmony* by the French composer Jean-Philippe Rameau.

When it comes to understanding the primary chords, many music theorists say that the interval of a perfect 5th is very important, for both historical and scientific/acoustic reasons. The root of the dominant harmony is a perfect 5th above the tonic, and the root of the subdominant harmony is a perfect 5th below the tonic (hence the name *sub*dominant).

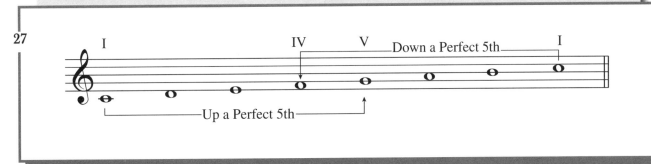

Three chords may not seem like much to work with, but thousands of songs are based on just I, IV and V.

The King's Singers originally billed themselves as the Schola Cantorum Pro Musica Profana in Cantabridgiense.

In terms of record sales, the group Boyz II Men is the most successful R&B act of all time.

CREATING CHORD PROGRESSIONS

A *chord progression* is a series of chords. The chords that accompany a song or are created by the vocal harmonies in a song are that song's chord progression. The most basic chord progression is I–IV–V–I. Theorists tell us that in our culture, we are conditioned to expect to hear the roots of chords move downward by a perfect 5th. From I to IV is root movement downward by a perfect 5th, and from V to I is root movement downward by a perfect 5th. That pretty well explains why I–IV–V–I is so prevalent in our music.

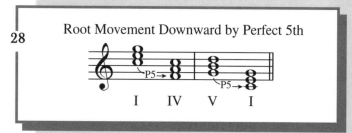

You could create thousands of harmony arrangements with just those three chords, but of course there are even more possibilities. Here's a way to stick with the *idea* of three primary harmonies, even while putting some others into your harmony arrangements.

Think of each of the three functions—tonic, subdominant and dominant—as being a club that other chords can join as long as they have two or more notes in common with the primary chord.

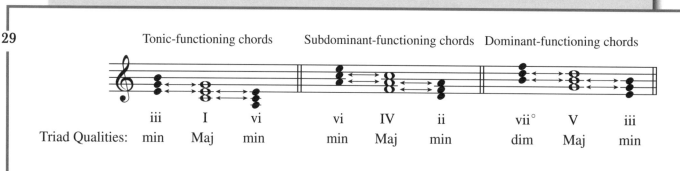

Notice that some of the chords can belong to more than one club. For example, vi can be thought of as functioning either as a tonic or as a subdominant. It all depends on the context. With this information, you can create I–IV–V–I progressions, substituting chords from the different catagories for the primary chords. Here are some examples, showing the chords in the key of C.

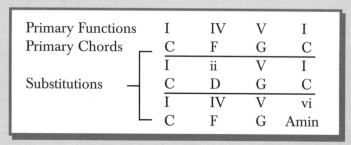

Have some fun making up your own versions of the I–IV–V–I progression. This is a great way to create new chord progressions that add interest to your harmony arrangements.

Some musicians love to turn things around and break with convention. Chord progressions that change the traditional order of the harmonies, such as V–IV–I or I–IV–V–IV, and so on, are common. Experiment!

USING THREE VOICES

In this arrangement of "America the Beautiful," the middle voice has the melody line, supported by the bottom line, which uses the same rhythms. The top voice provides a countermelody, and all three voices combine to form good-sounding harmonies. To give you some harmonic guideposts, the primary chords are shown above the music. (Some of the V chords are actually dominant 7 chords, which we'll look at in more detail on page 45.)

AMERICA THE BEAUTIFUL

Katherine Lee Bates
Samuel Augustus Ward

In three-part arrangements, there are a number of possibilities for using different textures and types of motion. One of the commonest ways to combine three voices is *block style,* in which all parts move at the same time (with the same exact rhythms), creating a dense sound that reinforces the melody. Example 30 introduces *minor keys.* This example is in F♯ Minor, which uses the same key signature as A Major. However, F♯ is the tonic, and the resulting scale and chords have a darker sound than the major keys we've already looked at. Also notice the use of inversion; for example, all of the triads in the last two measures are in second inversion.

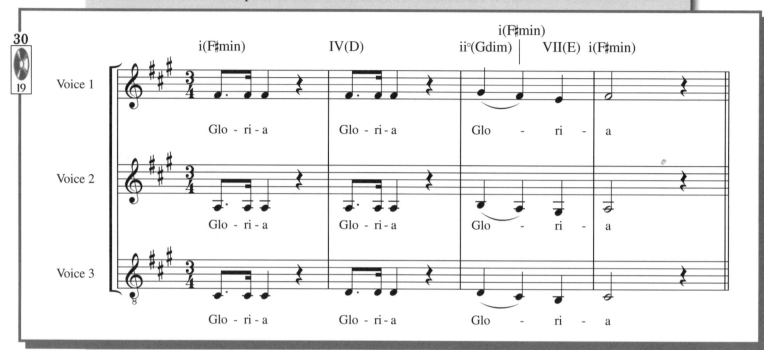

Example 31 is in a more contrapuntal style; notice how each voice is treated as a more or less independent unit. Though each voice has its own shape and character, all three work together to create solid harmonies that support the main line.

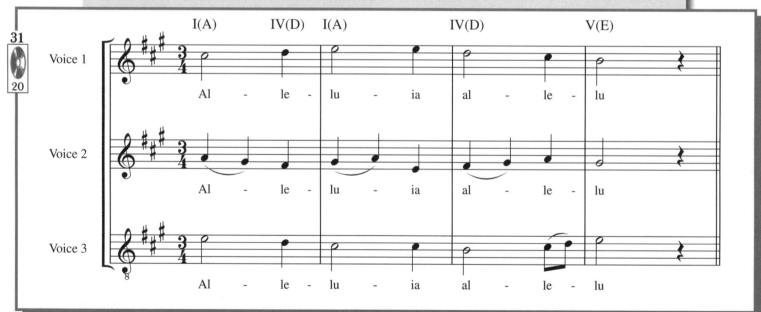

NONHARMONIC TONES

In the three-part examples we've looked at so far, the individual parts have in most cases added up to chordal harmonies—that is, the sound you hear at any moment is the sound of a chord. In making arrangements, however, you can also use *nonharmonic tones*—notes that don't function as part of a chord, but which add color and interest to an arrangement. Depending on the context, nonharmonic tones can be used to smooth out transitions from one note to another in a line, or as pure decoration. Generally, different types of nonharmonic tones are used in different ways, and each has certain guidelines for use. Here are the most common nonharmonic tones you'll encounter.

A *passing tone* is a nonharmonic tone that comes between two chord tones a third apart, filling in the gap between them. Passing tones are approached and left by step, always in the same direction.

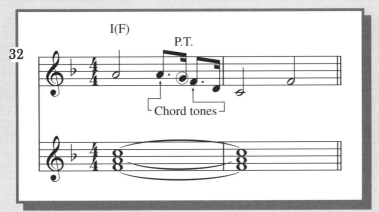

P.T. = Passing Tone

A *neighboring tone* is a nonharmonic tone a half step or whole step away that comes between two occurrences of the same chord tone. Neighboring tones are approached and left by step, always in different directions. If the neighboring tone is lower than the chord tone, it is called a *lower neighbor*. If the neighboring tone is higher than the chord tone, it is called an *upper neighbor*.

L.N. = Lower Neighbor
U.N. = Upper Neighbor

A *suspension* is a chord tone that is held across a change of harmony and then resolves by step to a chord tone in the new harmony. In most cases, a suspension happens on a strong beat (for example, beats 1 and 3 in $\frac{4}{4}$).

Every suspension has three parts: the *preparation,* the suspension itself, and the *resolution.* Take a look at example 35. In the first measure, the top note, C, is a member of the C Major chord; this is the preparation. Continuing to the *downbeat* (first beat) of the next measure, this C is held over the change of chord from C Major to G Major; this is the suspension. On beat two of the same measure, this C resolves downward to B, which is a member of the G Major chord; this is the resolution.

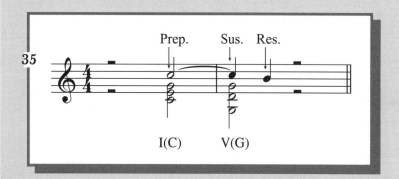

Prep. = Preparation
Sus. = Suspension
Res. = Resolution

An *anticipation* is a chord tone that sounds before (anticipates) the change of harmony to that chord.

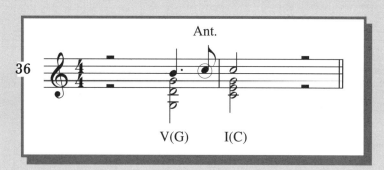

Ant. = Anticipation

An *appoggiatura* is a nonharmonic tone that is approached by skip and then resolves by step to a chord tone.

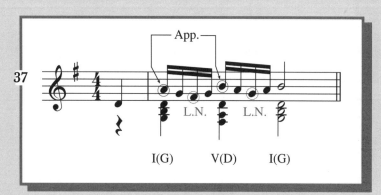

App. = Appoggiatura

An *escape tone* is a nonharmonic tone that is approached by step and then resolves by skip to a chord tone.

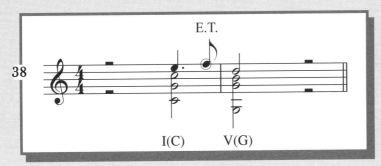

E.T. = Escape Tone

A *pedal point* is a tone that is either held or sounded repeatedly through several chord changes and is a member of the last chord that sounds with it.

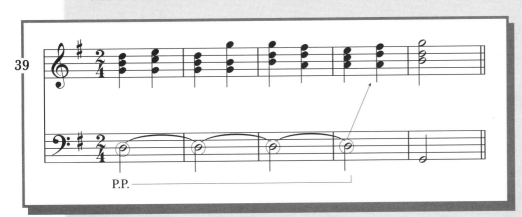

P.P. = Pedal Point

At the time they made their first recording, "Surfin'," in 1961, the Beach Boys billed themselves as the Pendletones.

Using a principle called multiphonics, some singers are actually able to harmonize with themselves by producing two notes at once. However, the "extra" note is almost never as clear or pure as the first.

NONHARMONIC TONES: REVIEW WORKSHEET

Circle and label the nonharmonic tone in each example.

Passing Tone (P.T.)

Suspension (Sus.)

Upper Neighbor (U.N.)

Lower Neighbor (L.N.)

Anticipation (Ant.)

Escape Tone (E.T.)

Appoggiatura (App.)

Pedal Point (P.P.)

Answers:

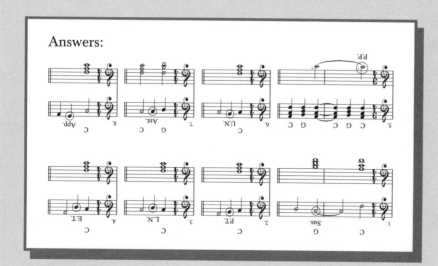

"Swing Low, Sweet Chariot" uses three different triads: F Major, B♭ Major and C Major. Notice that in some cases—for example, the syllable "ot" in measure 2—not all the notes of a harmony will change at exactly the same time. Also, as on the same syllable "ot," one note may be left out of a triad, and one of the remaining notes will be doubled (from the bottom up, B♭–B♭–D moving to A–A–C).

Find one lower neighboring tone and one upper neighboring tone in "Swing Low, Sweet Chariot." (Hint: One is in Voice 1, and one is in Voice 3.) The answers are at the bottom of the page.

SWING LOW, SWEET CHARIOT

ANSWERS:

The D in measure 4 of Voice 1 is an upper neighbor. The E in measure 5 of Voice 3 is a lower neighbor.

CHAPTER 6
FOUR-PART HARMONY

FOUR-PART GUIDELINES

As we saw with the three-part arrangements in chapter 5, vocal lines can be combined in any manner, as long as the harmonies and use of nonharmonic tones make sense. The same rules apply to four-part harmony, though the additional voice opens up new possibilities for texture and harmony.

Let's take a look at some basic guidelines in four-part harmony.

1. It's generally best to avoid having the bass move in similar motion with the melody or upper parts.

2. Only rarely should all four voices move in the same direction at the same time.

3. Consistent use of parallel and/or similar motion lessens the sense of independence among the lines.

4. Using unisons, octaves and 5ths in parallel motion lessens the sense of independence among the lines and is generally avoided.

5. Use a complete chord (that is, don't leave any notes out) wherever possible. When using triads, it's best to double the root when possible. If a note must be omitted, leave out the 5th of the chord.

6. Avoid doubling the seventh degree of the scale and any notes that have been *chromatically* altered—that is, notes that have been changed by an accidental.

7. Avoid overlapping or crossing voices. For example, in most cases, the notes in one voice part shouldn't be higher than those in the next higher part.

8. It's generally best to maintain the interval of an octave or less between adjacent voice parts (for example, soprano/alto and alto/tenor). The exception to this guideline is the two bottom voices (in four-part writing, usually tenor/bass), in which the interval may be greater.

9. Strive for a balanced mixture of similar, contrary, oblique and parallel motion among the parts.

7TH CHORDS

Now that you have four-voice textures at your disposal, let's take a look at some of the most common four-note chords. *7th chords* add a fourth note, a 7th above the root, to the triads you already know. (In fact, you can also use 7th chords in three-voice textures: Just leave out the 5th of the chord.) While a number of different 7th chords are possible, we'll focus on the most common types.

The *major 7th chord* is made up of the major scale degrees 1, 3, 5 and 7. For a major 7th chord built on C, the symbol is "CMaj7."

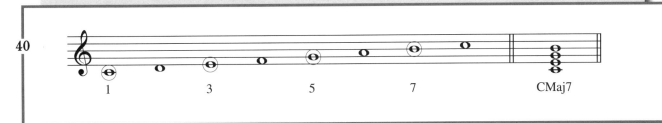

The *dominant 7th chord* is made up of the major scale degrees 1, 3, 5 and flat 7 ($^\flat$7). For a dominant 7th chord build on C, the symbol is "C7."

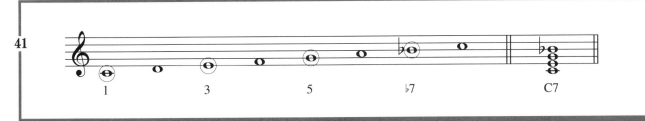

The *minor 7th chord* is made up of the major scale degrees 1, $^\flat$3, 5 and $^\flat$7. For a minor 7th chord built on C, the symbol is "Cmin7."

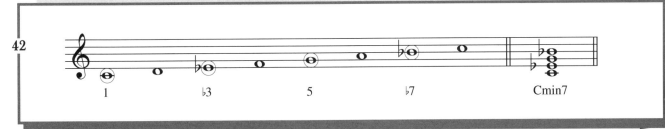

The name of the group Martha and the Vandellas was inspired by the Detroit thoroughfare Van Dyke Road and singer/actress Della Reese.

Before earning fame as a composer of choral music, Carlo Gesualdo (about 1561–1613) was better known for having murdered his wife and her lover.

The *half diminished 7th chord* (often called minor 7 flat 5) is made up of the major scale degrees 1, ♭3, ♭5 and ♭7. For a half diminished 7th chord built on C, the symbol is "Cmin7♭5." The half diminished 7th chord is also shown by a small circle with a diagonal line (ø7).

The *fully diminished 7th chord* (also called diminished 7) is made up of the major scale degrees 1, ♭3, ♭5 and double-flatted 7 (♭♭7)*. For a fully diminished 7th chord built on C, the symbol is "Cdim7." The fully diminished 7th chord is also sometimes shown with a small circle (°7).

> *♭♭ = *Double flat.* Double flatting lowers a note by two half steps (or one whole step). In a major scale, the ♭♭7 scale degree is the same pitch as the 6th scale degree, and, for ease of reading, is sometimes spelled as 6 rather than ♭♭7.
>
> B♭♭ = A

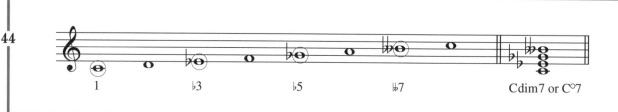

Below are the diatonic 7th chords for the major scale. Seventh chords are most often used in the context of a dominant function (as in V7 or vii°7), but any diatonic 7th chord can be called into service, and any type of 7th chord can be constructed on any scale degree. In jazz, for example, the other diatonic 7th chords are often used as characteristic "color" chords. In the end, your ears will tell you which 7th chords work well and which ones don't in a given musical context.

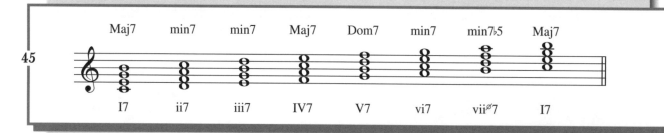

Maj7	=	Major 7th chord
min7	=	minor 7th chord
Dom7	=	Dominant 7th chord
ø7	=	Half diminished 7th chord

Look at the different ways in which the voices are used in the four-part arrangements of "Alleluja" and "The Heavens Are Telling" below. In "Alleluja," the alto moves mainly in parallel 3rds with the soprano, reinforcing the soprano's melody, while the male voices fill out the harmony with a simpler rhythm of their own. In "The Heavens Are Telling," all four voices sing nearly identical rhythms throughout, though each part has a more independent melodic shape. Notice the use of diatonic 7th chords in "Alleluja."

LEARNING TO SING FOUR-PART ARRANGEMENTS

Pages 48–58 contain complete four-part vocal arrangements. Once you find the part that best suits your voice range and have learned and memorized it, try singing along with the other parts on the CD. Here are a few observations and suggestions you might find helpful:

1. The melody in each arrangement is in the soprano line.

2. If the key of any of these arrangements is too high or low for your voice, it may be possible to *transpose* (change the key of) the arrangement. Experienced keyboard accompanists can often transpose on the spot, while guitarists can easily transpose to a higher key by using a device called a *capo*. If you perform these *a cappella* (without instrumental accompaniment) with other singers, you can transpose by shifting each part's first note up or down by the exact same interval. Since, if you transpose correctly, the interval relationships remain the same throughout a piece, you can simply transpose the first chord as needed and continue as you would in the original key. In the example below, the opening C Major chord has been transposed up to D Major by moving each part's note up by a whole step. From this new opening chord, the singers can continue as normal, but the piece will sound in the new, higher key. Notice that the key signature has changed to reflect the new, higher key.

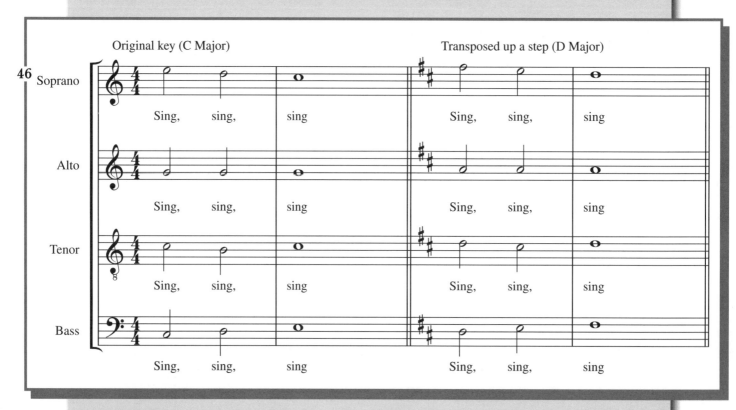

3. Sometimes, it's easier to learn your part if you first sing or hum it on a neutral syllable such as "la" instead of singing the words.

4. If you lose your place, drop out until you find your way back. In most cases, the other three parts will continue to sound well together even without the fourth part. It will sound like a mistake only if you stop and let the song fall apart. Remember that the show must go on!

WHEN THE SAINTS GO MARCHING IN

Traditional

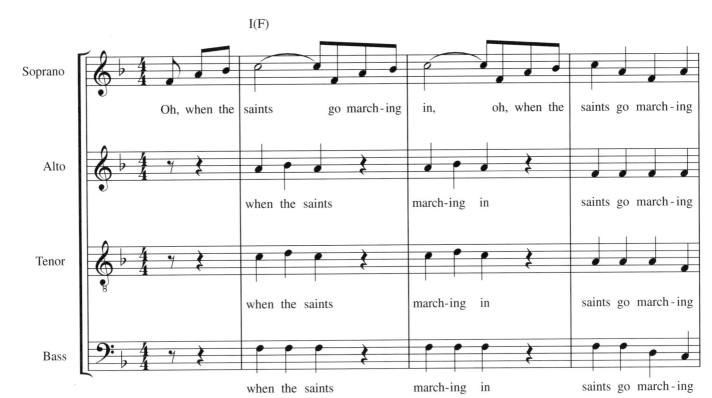

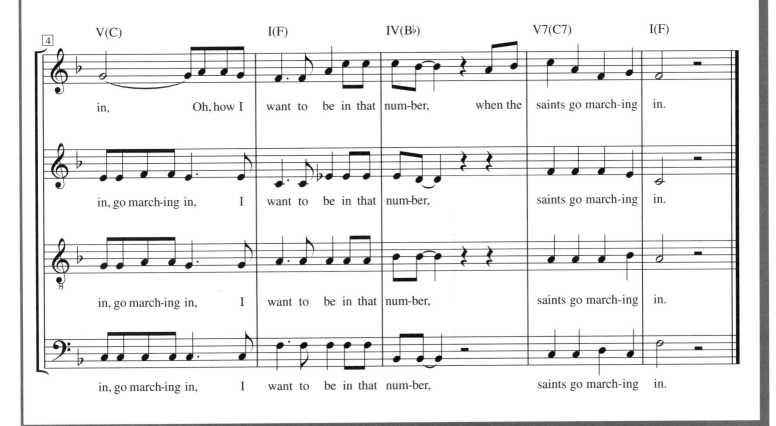

AMAGING GRACE

Traditional

* V7/IV = V7 of IV. This is an example of a *secondary dominant*. A secondary dominant is a dominant 7th–sounding chord with a root a 5th above (or a 4th below) a diatonic chord. So, as in this example, the D7 chord on beat 1 of measure 2 is "applied" to the following chord, G, as the V7 of that chord—that is, V7 of IV.

SILENT NIGHT

Franz Gruber
Joseph Mohr

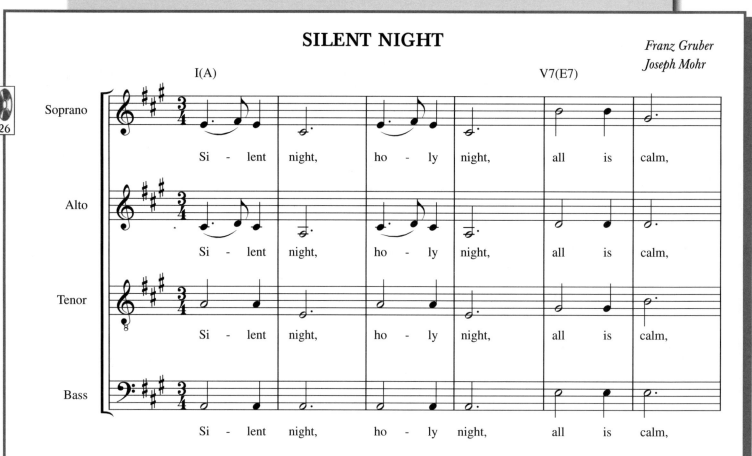

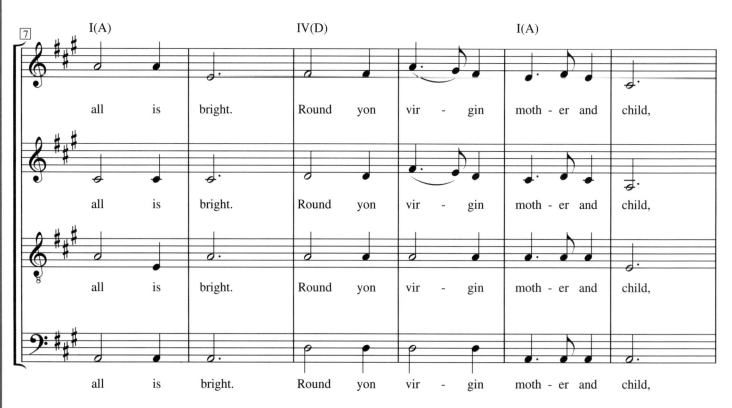

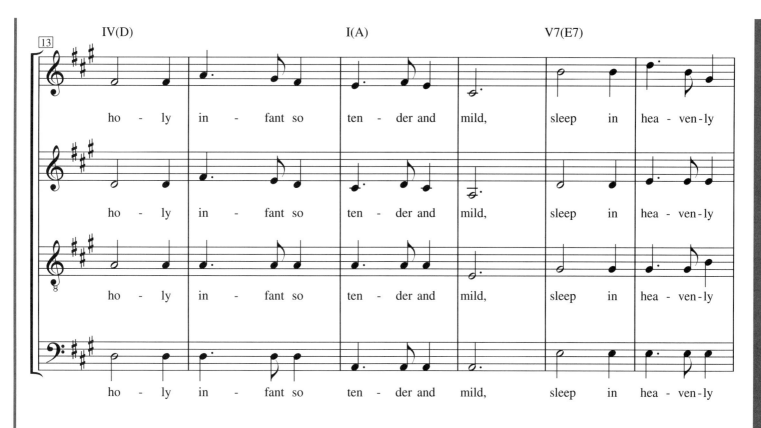

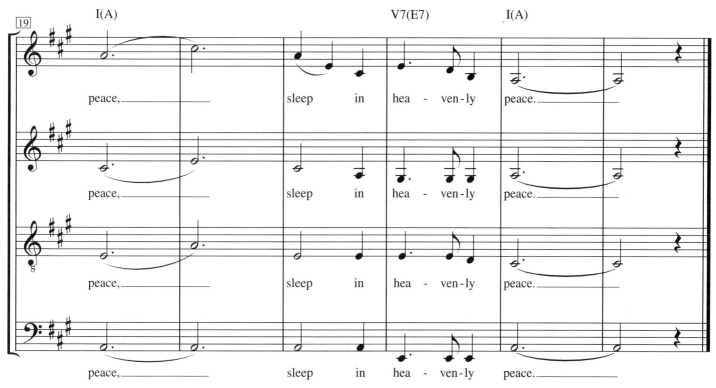

"The Water Is Wide" uses *syncopation,* which is the shifting of accents to the offbeat. One of the most common syncopations occurs when a note is played on the offbeat or "and" count and is held through the following strong beat. This is often called an *anticipation* (similar to the anticipation you learned about on page 40), since the note is sounded before it is expected. For example, the word "wide" in the first measure falls on the "and" of beat four, and is held over into the next measure.

THE WATER IS WIDE

Traditional

Notice in this version of "All Through the Night" that not all of the voices are used all of the time. One thing to keep in mind when you make your own arrangements is that singers need to breathe, and they appreciate moments of rest. Using the voices in various combinations also lends more variety to an arrangement. Here, the soprano sings the melody against a countermelody in either the tenor or the alto, while all four voices come together in a fuller texture on the words "all through the night."

ALL THROUGH THE NIGHT

Traditional

"Keep Your Lamps Trimmed and Burning" is in E Minor, which has the same key signature as G Major; however, E is the tonic.

KEEP YOUR LAMPS TRIMMED AND BURNING

Traditional

CANONS AND ROUNDS

A *canon* is a piece or passage in which a single melody is imitated, at the same or a different pitch, by voices that enter at different times. A *round* is a type of short *perpetual canon* (a repeatedly cycling canon) in which the voices sing the melody at the unison or octave. Singing canons and rounds is good practice for holding on to your own vocal part while hearing another part at the same time.

In the four-part round "Are You Sleeping?" (the English-language version of "Frère Jacques"), the entrances of the different voices are marked by numbers above the staff. The first voice enters at ①. At ②, the first voice continues, and the second voice begins the song. When the first voice reaches ③, the two voices continue, and the third voice begins the song. When the first voice reaches ④, the three voices continue, and the fourth voice begins the song. The four voices can continue to cycle through the song a predetermined number of times or as long as their lungs hold out.

ARE YOU SLEEPING?

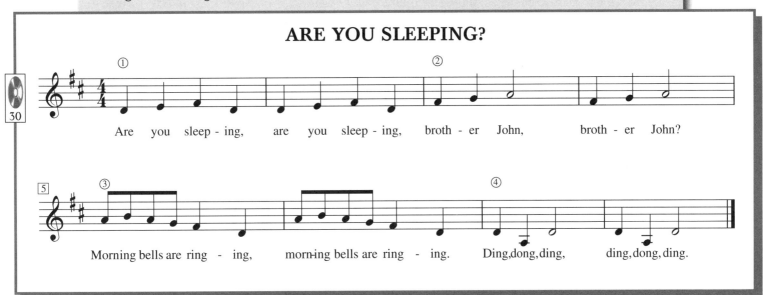

OSTINATOS

An *ostinato* is a repeated, usually short figure sung against a melody. Sometimes, ostinatos are extracted directly from the melody. Ostinatos can make an interesting introduction or conclusion to a song, and several ostinatos can even be sung or played simultaneously.

Let's try adding an ostinato to "Frère Jacques." While the other parts sing in canon, another voice will sing this ostinato:

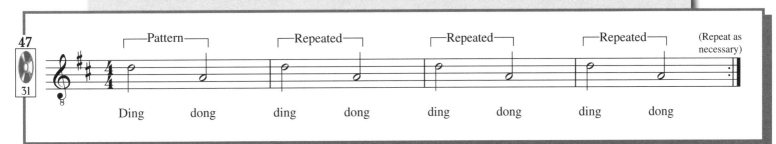

CHAPTER 7
CREATING AND PRACTICING VOCAL HARMONY

SPONTANEOUS HARMONY SINGING

All the tips you've learned about harmony singing so far will be helpful when you have the time to practice and polish your harmony singing with another singer. You'll sharpen your skills even more, though, by learning to sing harmony on the fly (that is, spontaneously) with another singer or even with a recording. Here are some tips to get you started, followed by some arrangements on pages 61–64 that will give you some ideas for improvising vocal harmony.

1. **Singing up a 3rd.** At your next sing-along, try singing along with the melody at the interval of a 3rd above. To find your starting note, sing up two scale degrees from the starting note of the melody. By maintaining this distance above the melody as you sing, you'll be harmonizing in 3rds. Depending on the notes involved, the interval between the melody and your harmony line will vary between a major 3rd and a minor 3rd, creating a natural, pleasing effect. You may need to adjust the interval according to the chord that is involved. Just use your ears, and let your voice follow the flow of the melody.

2. **Singing down a 3rd.** Harmonizing a 3rd below a melody works the same way as harmonizing a 3rd above, only the voices are reversed—that is, the melody is on top, and the harmony is below. To find your starting note, sing down two scale degrees from the starting note of the melody. As before, the interval between the voices will vary between a major 3rd and a minor 3rd, and adjustments may sometimes be needed to create the best-sounding harmonies.

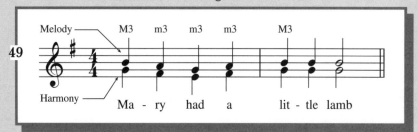

3. **Singing chord tones**. The effectiveness and ease of this technique depends on the song's *harmonic rhythm*—that is, the rate at which the chords change. Try singing a chord tone on the downbeat of each measure, and stay on this pitch until you hear the chord change. The root of the chord may be the easiest note to find at first, but you can create a smoother line by moving to the 3rd or 5th (when moving to a 5th, it's best to move in the opposite direction as the melody), depending on which is closest to the note you've just sung. Effectively harmonizing in this way takes some practice—it's generally easiest with a slow harmonic rhythm—but the more you do it, the greater the instinct you'll develop for anticipating chord changes. As you become more skilled, you'll be able to create accompaniments with greater variety and color.

Below and on page 62, you'll find three different harmonizations of the popular Christmas carol "The First Noel." In the first version, the bottom voice sings the melody, while the upper voice provides the harmony, mostly in 3rds.

THE FIRST NOEL I

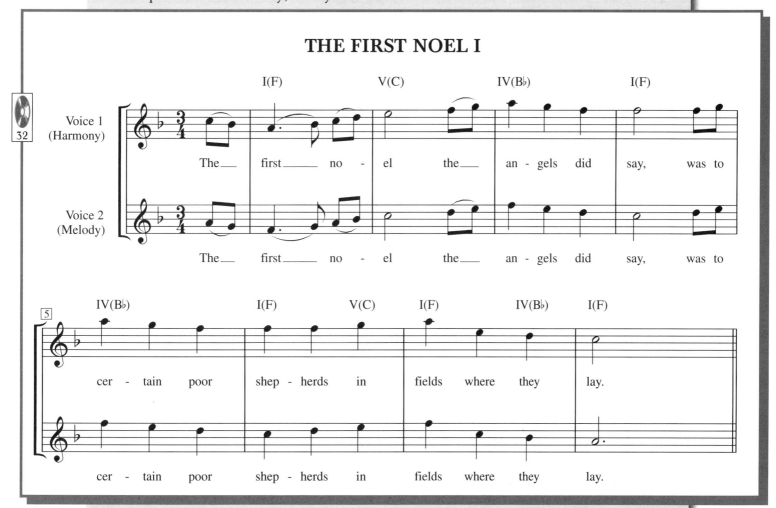

In this version of "The First Noel," the roles are reversed. The upper voice sings the melody, and the lower voice provides the harmony, mainly in 3rds.

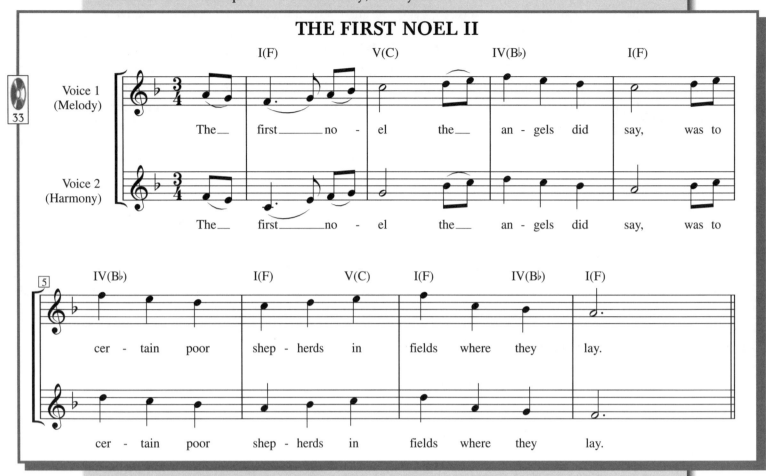

In this version of "The First Noel," the top voice sings the melody, and the bottom voice harmonizes by singing chord roots.

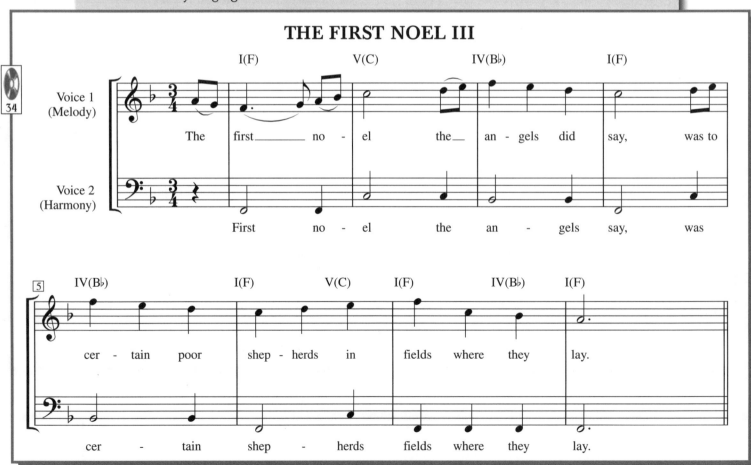

In this version of "Down by the Riverside," the bottom voice sings the melody, while the top voice provides the harmony.

DOWN BY THE RIVERSIDE I

This version of "Down by the Riverside" reverses the roles of voices in the version on page 63. The melody is in the top part, and the harmony is in the bottom part.

DOWN BY THE RIVERSIDE II

VOCAL EXERCISES IN HARMONY

The exercises on this page will help you sharpen the skills that are useful in creating a good harmony part. Example 51 will help you hear chord changes. Try singing each of the parts on the syllable "la"; for those that are too high or low, sing them in the octave that is most natural for you.

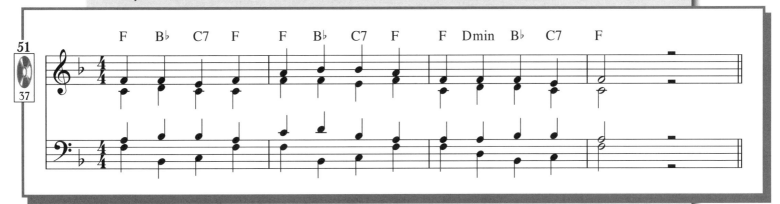

Example 52 will help you hear scale degrees. Practice each part using the given syllables. When you're ready to put the parts together, sing each note on the syllable "la."

In example 53, the lower part sings up and down the C Major scale, while the higher part sings the triad built on each scale degree. Use the syllable "la."

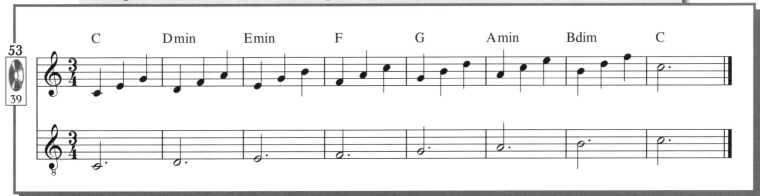

GUIDELINES FOR CREATING AN EFFECTIVE HARMONY PART

1. **Listen to yourself as well as to the other voices.** Listening to the overall texture—your own voice included—is essential not only for in-tune and rhythmically accurate singing, but also for creating a good *blend* (the overall effect of several voices singing at once).

2. **Follow the melody.** The melody line paves the way for the harmonies you provide. Hearing the movement and *contour* (shape) of the melody line is crucial when it comes to adding a harmony part. As you become more experienced, you'll even find yourself anticipating the movement of the melody.

3. **Be sensitive to phrasing, word placement and overall character.** Be sure to place syllables and to phrase your part (that is, create a complete musical thought as you sing as opposed to thinking in terms of one note at a time) in a way that is consistent with the other part(s). Listen carefully so that you and the other singers can make entrances, endings and cut-offs as clean and precise as possible.

   If one voice sings a passage with a distant, dreamy quality, while another voice sings the same passage as if it were a power ballad, the result will probably sound sloppy or careless. Follow the example of the lead singer when it comes to determining the character or atmosphere of a musical line or passage. Working out such details in advance, when possible, is probably the best solution of all. No musical element should be regarded as small or unimportant.

4. **Choose a good key.** Some songs may feel perfectly comfortable to sing in one key, while the same song in a higher or lower key feels completely different. If your part feels uncomfortably high or low in a particular key, try transposing the song up or down to a key that better suits your voice. One quick way to determine how well the key of a particular song will work for you is to scan the music to look for the hightest and lowest notes in your part, and adjust the key accordingly. When multiple voices are involved, some compromise may be necessary to best accommodate all of the singers.

5. **Practice.** It takes repetition and hard work to create a good harmony part. Sing your part slowly to ensure accuracy, record your part, and work on singing each pitch and rhythm precisely.

Early working titles for the classic musical West Side Story included East Side Story and Gangway.

Despite their massive popularity, ABBA made it to the top of the American charts only once, in 1977, with "Dancing Queen."

OPPORTUNITIES FOR HARMONY SINGING PRACTICE

As with any skill, practice makes perfect when it comes to harmony singing. Here are some possible opportunities to maintain and improve your singing and listening skills that you may not have thought of.

1. **Community choruses.** Look in newspapers for ads, audition dates and concerts given by local community choruses.

2. **Church choirs.** Church music has a centuries-old tradition of part-singing. Try contacting your church or religious institution about its choir's rehearsal and performance schedules.

3. **Regional and all-state music festivals and conferences.** High schools can often give you information about events of this type. Festivals often provide the opportunity to hear a variety of vocal ensembles. Organizations such as the American Choral Directors Association (ACDA) and the Music Educators National Conference (MENC) hold conferences and workshops on a regular basis.

4. **Library programs.** Some local libraries offer music-related lectures or classes.

5. **Holiday sing-alongs.** Use any chance you get to practice your harmony singing. Handel's oratorio *The Messiah* is a perennial favorite in many communities, and performing great works as part of a large group can be an unforgettable experience.

6. **Community theater.** Many local theater productions, especially musicals, make use of vocal soloists and ensembles. Check local newspapers for audition times and dates.

7. **Barbershop quartets.** Many barbershop quartets and similar ensembles for female voices, such as the Sweet Adelines, are part of larger national and international organizations, which you can locate on-line.

8. **Private lessons.** Taking private voice lessons is probably the best way to receive individual attention as you begin to learn harmony singing. Music stores and music departments of colleges are usually very helpful in referring students and teachers to one another. Talk with several teachers, be sure to clearly outline your goals, and ask a lot of questions. This is probably the best way to find a teacher who will be compatible with you.

CHAPTER 8
CREATING VOCAL HARMONY ARRANGEMENTS

GUIDELINES FOR CREATING AN EFFECTIVE VOCAL ARRANGEMENT

1. **Study**. One of the best ways to learn how to create an effective vocal arrangement is to study some effective vocal arrangements. Find the scores of some pieces you especially like and follow along with them as you listen to the recording. As you listen, keep a mental (or even written) checklist of details. What kinds of harmonies are used? Does the texture remain the same throughout, or does it vary? How well does the music reflect the meaning of the words? Practice singing through the piece part by part—noting passages that seem especially well-written, challenging or quirky—and try to figure out what gives the arrangement its character.

2. **The importance of words.** The music should enhance—not obscure—the words. Since the parts sing the same words at the same time, block-chord textures are a good choice when maximum intelligibility of the words is important. At the same time, too much of the same thing can quickly become boring. Think about varying the texture (for example, by using different combinations of voices) and the rhythmic alignment of the parts, even slightly, to provide extra interest. Counterpoint can be used to great effect, but be aware that greater independence of individual parts often means that the words are harder to understand.

3. **Think possible and practical.** Make sure that each part is singable and makes musical sense. A good rule of thumb is to keep individual lines as smooth and melodic as possible. The best way to test the effectiveness of individual parts is to sing through them yourself. If you find that a part you've written is easy and comfortable to sing and works well for the voice, chances are you've written a good part. If you find that a part is awkward and uncomfortable, chances are it needs more work.

4. **Be clear.** Since others will have to read from your arrangement, be sure to make your notation clear and precise. Don't forget to use the proper clef for each voice part. (For a review of the different vocal clefs, see page 21.)

5. **Be thorough.** Remember that every musical decision you *don't* make must be made by some-one else. Be sure that your musical intentions are clearly spelled out in your arrangements.

6. **Support your singers**. Instrumental support is extremely useful for good *intonation* (tuning). Instrumental support can be as simple as doubling each part on an instrument or having an instrument play chords. Depending on your abilities or background, you can create a more complex accompaniment that, while helping the singers, also has a personality of its own.

7. **Use melodic intervals carefully.** Certain melodic intervals should be used with special caution. The augmented 4th/diminished 5th can be particularly hard to sing in tune, as are large intervals—that is, those larger than a 6th. One principle to remember as you make arrangements is that problems that might be slight for one singer are often compounded when more voices are involved.

8. **Use harmonic intervals carefully.** In two-part textures, 3rds and 6ths are almost always effective as harmonic intervals. Be careful when using dissonant intervals (2nds and 7ths) and when using 4ths or 5ths, which can produce a hollow or "medieval" effect when used to excess. Be sure to use dissonances and nonharmonic tones properly, according to the guidelines on pages 39–41.

WRITING YOUR OWN HARMONY

We'll explore one approach to writing a harmony part by completing the arrangement of "Clementine" on page 70. First, look at the melody line, which in this case is in the bottom part. Sing the notes of the melody one by one, concentrating on the direction the line takes. Take note of the chord changes; when working with printed music that doesn't include chord changes, try out different possibilities.

Once you have the melody part and chords, it's time to write the harmony. Look at the first chord in the song, and write down which notes it contains. In "Clementine," the first chord is G Major (G–B–D). To fill in the harmony parts, find the remaining chord tones above the first melody note. The melody of "Clementine," sung by Voice 3, begins on G, the root. The next note of the chord is B, the 3rd, which is the starting note for Voice 1. This leaves the 5th of the chord, D, for the remaining harmony part (Voice 2).

Use the same procedure on every note of the melody. When the chords change, so will the notes used in creating the harmony parts. In the fourth full measure of "Clementine," the chord changes to D Major (D–F♯–A). Here, the melody note is A. The closest chord tone above it is D, while the closest below it is F♯. These are the harmony notes you'll use for the first beat of that measure.

The melody of "Clementine" uses all chord tones, with two exceptions. The first is a passing tone (C) in measure 3; the second is another passing tone (B) in measure 5. Notice in the first instance that the corresponding harmony parts also use passing tones at this point.

Now, try completing the harmony parts for the last four measures of "Clementine," using the skills that you've learned. While there is no one right way to complete this exercise, be sure to apply the principles you learned on pages 66 and 68 and elsewhere in the book. When you've finished, try out each part by playing or singing it, and make adjustments accordingly. Once you've completed the arrangement, try performing it with other singers, and listen with a critical ear, taking note of both the most effective and least effective elements.

Francis Hopkinson (1737–1791), often credited as America's first songwriter, was also a signer of the Declaration of Independence and designer of the American flag sewn by Betsy Ross.

The Motown trio the Supremes began as a quartet called the Primettes.

CLEMENTINE

Traditional

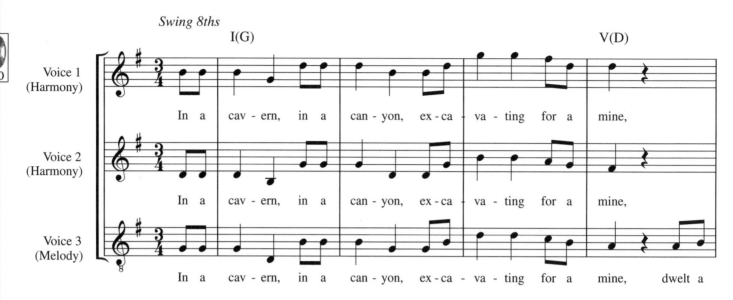

Voice 1 (Harmony): In a cav - ern, in a can - yon, ex - ca - va - ting for a mine,

Voice 2 (Harmony): In a cav - ern, in a can - yon, ex - ca - va - ting for a mine,

Voice 3 (Melody): In a cav - ern, in a can - yon, ex - ca - va - ting for a mine, dwelt a

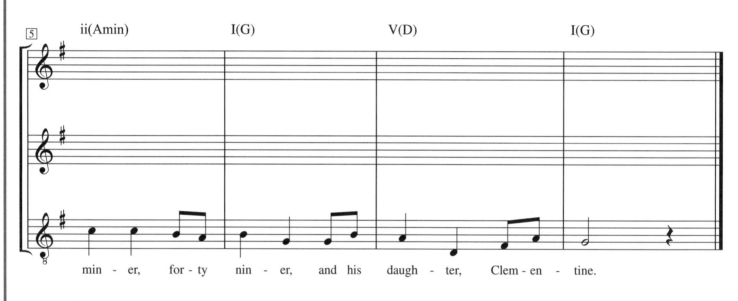

min - er, for - ty nin - er, and his daugh - ter, Clem - en - tine.

The Righteous Brothers hit "Unchained Melody" was written by Alex North, a composer best known for such film scores as A Streetcar Named Desire and Spartacus.

Three of the greatest masters of Baroque vocal music—Bach, Handel, and Scarlatti—were all born in 1685.

Use the same procedure you used with "Clementine" to provide harmony parts for "Red River Valley." Have the harmony parts rest for the pickup, and bring them in for the first full measure.

RED RIVER VALLEY

Traditional

CHAPTER 9
VOCAL MUSIC HISTORY AND ARTISTS

Now that you've learned some fundamentals, let's pause to look back at the history of vocal music. Knowing something about the history of vocal music will not only help you broaden your musical horizons, but may even lend you some inspiration and fresh ideas when you begin to make your own arrangements. One important thing to remember is that most often, there are no neat boundaries between different periods and styles, so the given dates for each period should be regarded only as approximations.

MIDDLE AGES/MEDIEVAL PERIOD (800–1450)
CHARACTERISTICS
During the Middle Ages, music in churches and monasteries consisted of settings taken from the scriptures. This period saw the birth of countless *monophonic* (single-line) chants, which were largely passed on through oral tradition. Pope Gregory arranged to have these chants written down and collected in about 590, and they have come to be known as *Gregorian chants*. Gregory's efforts played a central role in the spread of this music throughout Europe, and Gregorian chant (or *plainchant*) came to represent the first great pillar of the Western musical tradition.

Gregorian chant is marked by flowing, natural rhythms (shown by a lack of barlines in modern notation) and simple, mostly stepwise motion, and is generally performed a cappella. Chants were constructed from *modes* (stepwise reorderings of the pitches in a scale), which eventually evolved into the system of *tonality* (keys) as we know it. Later in the medieval period, it became commonplace to add one or more instrumental parts—sometimes doubling the voices, sometimes providing a more distinctive accompaniment—to other types of vocal music.

Secular (non-sacred) vocal music in the Middle Ages is perhaps best represented by the humorous, amorous, even erotic songs of traveling singers/poets/players known variously as *jongleurs, troubadours* or *trouvères*. Though it isn't known exactly when part-singing began, it is believed that it was used in secular song before it was used in church music. In the earliest type of part-singing, two voices moved in parallel motion (usually in 4ths or 5ths) in a technique called *organum*. By the 13th century, added voices took on a more independent character, marked by the use of long-held rhythms against a more active melodic part. From that point, composers began to combine voices in myriad ways, both refining older traditions and developing new ones. As the Renaissance dawned in the 15th century, contrapuntal vocal music had evolved into a sophisticated art that produced vocal music of unprecedented complexity and presented composers with a staggering variety of possibilities.

SOME IMPORTANT COMPOSERS OF MUSIC FOR THE VOICE
Guiraut de Bornelh (1173–1220)

Léonin (early to mid-1200s)

Petrus de Cruce (active ca. 1270–1300)

Philippe de Vitry (1291–1361)

Guillaume de Machaut (ca. 1300–1377)

Francesco Landini (ca. 1350–1397)

Ca. = *Circa.* Approximately

RENAISSANCE PERIOD (1450–1600)

CHARACTERISTICS

With its rich legacy of vocal music, the Renaissance is widely regarded as the golden period of a cappella singing. Vocal music in the Renaissance ranged from songs for a single voice and *lute* (a stringed and fretted plucked instrument) to elaborate choral settings with four, five, six and even more parts.

Renaissance vocal music was notated without explicit time signatures. Choral settings were often quite elaborate, incorporating mainly stepwise motion, imitation and a variety of textures, often within the course of a single work. Two of the most important vocal genres were the *madrigal* (an unaccompanied, usually secular piece for multiple voices) and the *motet* (an unaccompanied, usually sacred work for multiple voices). Political and religious conflicts in Europe had a direct influence on vocal styles. While the simplification and "purification" of church music was one of the aims of the Protestant Reformation, Counter-Reformation composers such as Giovanni Pierluigi da Palestrina and Tomás Luis de Victoria lifted vocal counterpoint to new heights, producing some of the most lush and complex choral music ever written.

SOME IMPORTANT COMPOSERS OF MUSIC FOR THE VOICE

Johannes Ockeghem (ca. 1410–1497)

Josquin Desprez (ca. 1440–1521)

Clément Janequin (1485–1558)

Giovanni Pierluigi da Palestrina (ca. 1525–1594)

Orlande de Lassus (1532–1594)

William Byrd (1543–1623)

Tomás Luis de Victoria (1548–1611)

Giovanni Gabrieli (ca. 1555–1612)

Thomas Morley (ca. 1557–1602)

Carlo Gesualdo (ca. 1561–1613)

Palestrina was fired from his job as a singer in the Sistine Chapel because he got married. Palestrina's boss at the time? The pope.

Giovanni Gabrieli died in 1612 from complications arising from a kidney stone.

BAROQUE PERIOD (1600–1750)

CHARACTERISTICS

With the arrival of the Baroque period, vocal music reached new dramatic heights, aided by a number of innovations. Texts took on greater importance, evidenced in the development of *opera* (a sung and staged drama). Composers began to make explicit use of dynamics, and vocalists introduced *ornamentation* (an often improvised embellishment of a line) into their performances—sometimes, to excess. Though the principles behind keys had been taking shape for centuries, it was during the Baroque period that the system of keys and key signatures as we now know it was codified. Bass lines (vocal and otherwise) became increasingly important as a foundation and support for the expanding harmonic language used by composers.

The development of opera during the Baroque revolutionized the way vocal music was written and sung. The *aria* (a work for solo voice and instrumental accompaniment, typically part of an opera) gained particular popularity, and, more than any other genre, demonstrated the virtuosic possibilities of the human voice. Though all manner of *contrapuntal* (using counterpoint or multiple independent parts) writing flourished throughout the Baroque period, one of the most important vocal genres to reach its pinnacle was the *chorale* (a usually contrapuntal hymn setting). Chorales, which originated in Protestant church music in the sixteenth century, were typically written for four voice parts. The undisputed master of chorale writing was Johann Sebastian Bach, who produced hundreds of examples. Other choral genres that came into full flower during this era are the *cantata* (a dramatic work made up of a variety of solos and ensembles with instrumental accompaniment) and the *oratorio* (similar to an opera, but usually religious in subject matter and performed without staging).

SOME IMPORTANT COMPOSERS OF MUSIC FOR THE VOICE

Claudio Monteverdi (1567–1643)

Jean-Baptiste Lully (1632–1687)

Johann Pachelbel (1653–1706)

Henry Purcell (1659–1695)

Antonio Vivaldi (1678–1741)

Georg Philipp Telemann (1681–1767)

Jean-Philippe Rameau (1683–1764)

Georg Frideric Handel (1685–1759)

Johann Sebastian Bach (1685–1750)

Domenico Scarlatti (1685–1757)

Johann Sebastian Bach *(1685–1750)*
was one of the leading lights of
the Baroque era.

CLASSICAL PERIOD (1750–1825)

CHARACTERISTICS

The Classical period is often characterized as one of balance and formality, elegance and restraint. During this time, composers began to make particular use of large-scale, multi-sectional instrumental forms such as the *sonata* and *symphony,* which are marked by special attention to proportion and order. Composers began to use more detailed indications for dynamics and tempo, and the harmonic language continued to expand.

Vocal genres that had emerged during the Baroque—opera, oratorio and others—were further developed, and writing for voices became ever more complex and virtuosic, particularly in opera. The undisputed master of Classical opera was Wolfgang Amadeus Mozart, who produced such masterpieces as *The Marriage of Figaro, Don Giovanni* and *The Magic Flute.* Mozart's operas are distinguished not only by the composer's tuneful style, but also by his mastery in deftly combining solo arias, duets, trios and larger ensembles to dramatic ends. Earlier song traditions began to give way to the *art song* or *lied* (pronounced "leed"; German for "song"), a poetic setting for solo voice with solo instrumental (usually keyboard) accompaniment. In the fledgling United States, such composers as William Billings laid the foundations for an American vocal tradition, primarily through his hymns and *fuging tunes,* pieces for multiple voices that combine *homophonic* (chordal) and canon-like sections.

SOME IMPORTANT COMPOSERS OF MUSIC FOR THE VOICE

Jean-Jacques Rousseau (1712–1778)

Christoph Willibald Gluck (1714–1787)

Franz Joseph Haydn (1732–1809)

William Billings (1746–1800)

Wolfgang Amadeus Mozart (1756–1791)

Ludwig van Beethoven (1770–1827)

***Ludwig van Beethoven** (1770–1827) created a sensation by using voices in the final movement of his Symphony No. 9 (1824).*

ENGRAVING FROM *LIFE OF BEETHOVEN* BY LOUIS NOHL, TRANS. BY JOHN J. LALOR (CHICAGO: A. C. MCCLURG & CO., 1889)

ROMANTIC PERIOD (1825–1900)

CHARACTERISTICS

One important characteristic associated with music of the Classical period is a sense of order and clarity. Music of the Romantic period, on the other hand, has come to be more closely associated with unrestrained emotion, with feeling rather than intellect. Melodies took on a new, soaring freedom. The harmonic language became more adventurous to the point that the sense of tonality in works by such composers as Richard Wagner and Fránz Liszt all but disappeared.

The Romantic period opened the great age of Italian opera, as evidenced in the works of Gioachino Rossini, Vincenzo Bellini, Giuseppe Verdi and others. French and German opera also flourished, and the works of German composer Wagner in particular may be thought of as representing a one-man revolution in opera. Some composers, notably Felix Mendelssohn, looked to historical models in producing large-scale choral works in the spirit of Bach. The *requiem mass* (a church service for the dead), which had been around for centuries, reached new and richly varied heights of expression in works by Giuseppe Verdi, Hector Berlioz, Johannes Brahms, Gabriel Fauré and others. Both instrumental and choral ensembles swelled in size, at times (mostly for concerts marking special occasions) even numbering into the thousands of players and singers.

As large-scale choral works became even larger, smaller forms like the art song reached their pinnacle in the works of Franz Schubert, Robert Schumann, Johannes Brahms and others. Of central importance in the history of Romantic vocal music was the development of the *song cycle*, a collection of songs usually related by a single topic or even by an unfolding narrative. A cousin of the art song was the *parlor song*, a usually highly sentimental vocal setting with keyboard accompaniment that enjoyed particular popularity in the intimate settings of British and American homes.

SOME IMPORTANT COMPOSERS OF MUSIC FOR THE VOICE

Gioachino Rossini (1792–1868)

Franz Schubert (1797–1828)

Vincenzo Bellini (1801–1835)

Hector Berlioz (1803–1869)

Felix Mendelssohn (1809–1847)

Robert Schumann (1810–1856)

Richard Wagner (1813–1883)

Giuseppe Verdi (1813–1901)

Johannes Brahms (1833–1897)

Gabriel Fauré (1845–1924)

ENGRAVING FROM *LIFE OF WAGNER* BY LOUIS NOHL, TRANS. BY GEORGE P. UPTON (CHICAGO: A. C. MCCLURG & CO., 1889)

***Richard Wagner** (1813–1883) revolutionized the use of voices in such operas as* Tristan and Isolde *(1859) and* Parsifal *(1882).*

MODERN/CONTEMPORARY PERIOD (1900–PRESENT)

CHARACTERISTICS

The twentieth century was a time of wide-ranging experimentation in vocal music. While older genres like opera continued to flourish, they did so in the context of an ever-expanding musical language. Dissonance took on new expressive potential, composers approached rhythm and harmony with a new, anything-goes freedom, and more than ever, rules were made to be broken. New technologies ranging from sound recording to electronic instruments had a particular impact, inspiring composers to use the voice in ways that had never been imagined. The devastation wrought by the world wars proved a major influence on music, which began to reflect a new horror—and hope.

Its very diversity, more so than a "sound," is what gives twentieth-century vocal music its identity. The rich Romantic aesthetic was alive and well in the operas and art songs of composers like Richard Strauss, while other composers used the voice in ways that rendered it almost unrecognizable. Some composers wrote songs in the style of a hundred years earlier, while other composers dispensed with tonality altogether, writing music in which the idea of keys had no place. The mixing of popular and "serious" styles continued throughout the century. The line between opera and musical theater moved closer and closer together in works like George Gershwin's *Porgy and Bess* and Leonard Bernstein's *West Side Story.* "Serious" composers were influenced by jazz, jazz composers were influenced by classical music, and musicians as diverse as Duke Ellington and the Beatles earned the kind of respectability that few popular artists had ever enjoyed. (You can read more about popular twentieth-century artists on pages 77–90.)

With the arrival of the twenty-first century, developing technologies played an ever-increasing role in the creation and presentation of vocal music. Computers in particular opened up a whole new vista for composers and performers, making it possible for an individual to create sounds that had never been heard and to fit a recording studio and pressing plant into a space no larger than a desktop. Traditional definitions of opera, song and even of music itself found themselves challenged by more progressive musical imaginations.

SOME IMPORTANT COMPOSERS OF MUSIC FOR THE VOICE

Claude Debussy (1862–1918)

Arnold Schoenberg (1874–1951)

Béla Bartók (1881–1945)

Igor Stravinsky (1882–1971)

Sergei Prokofiev (1891–1953)

George Gershwin (1898–1937)

Kurt Weill (1900–1950)

Aaron Copland (1900–1990)

Benjamin Britten (1913–1976)

Leonard Bernstein (1918–1990)

George Gershwin *(1898–1937) wrote hundreds of songs, several hit musicals and the opera* Porgy and Bess *(1935).*

Now that we've made it up to the present day, let's take a closer look at some of the artists that shaped twentieth-century and contemporary vocal music.

THE ANDREWS SISTERS

The Andrews Sisters—Patty (born 1920), Maxene (1916–1995) and LaVerne (1911–1967)—began their musical careers while still in their teens. After touring with the Larry Rich Orchestra and performing in vaudeville, they signed their first record contract (with Decca) in 1937. In 1938, they had their first hit with "Bei Mir Bist Du Schön," which was also the first-ever million seller recorded by an all-female group. In the 1940s, and especially during World War II, the Andrews Sisters ruled America's radios and jukeboxes. Throughout the course of their career they performed with major artists like Bing Crosby and Glenn Miller, recorded more than 1,000 songs, sold more than 90 million records and appeared in 17 films.

The Andrews Sisters attained—and maintained—great popular success with a seemingly simple but effective formula: the combination of a wholesome image, a fresh, optimistic spirit and consummate vocal skill. As is the case in many musical groups, each of the sisters took on a different persona in the popular imagination. The Andrews Sisters' sound, marked by tightly knit vocals and closely spaced harmonies, was influenced in great part by the New Orleans trio the Boswell Sisters, and came to include many popular styles of the day, including swing and boogie-woogie.

LISTENING LIST
"Beer Barrel Polka (Roll out the Barrel)"

"Bei Mir Bist Du Schön"

"Boogie Woogie Bugle Boy"

"Don't Fence Me In"

"Don't Sit Under the Apple Tree"

"I'll Be with You in Apple Blossom Time"

"Pennsylvania 6–5000"

"Pistol Packin' Mama"

"Rum and Coca-Cola"

"Tuxedo Junction"

The Andrews Sisters scored their first number-one hit with *"Bei Mir Bist Du Schön" in 1938.*

PETER, PAUL AND MARY

Peter Yarrow (born 1938), Paul Stookey (born 1937) and Mary Travers (born 1937)—collectively, Peter, Paul and Mary—had their roots in such folk-oriented 1940s and 1950s groups as the Weavers, the Kingston Trio and the Highwaymen. After joining forces to perform in a New York coffeehouse in the early 1960s, the trio recorded their first, self-titled album in 1962. However, it was their second single, "If I Had a Hammer," that became their first bona fide hit and propelled them to national stardom. Peter, Paul and Mary's often politically charged and socially conscious music had a particular resonance with listeners in the turbulent 1960s, which helped the trio maintain a high profile throughout the decade. Though their popularity waned somewhat during the 1970s, they have continued to perform and record together to the present day, demonstrating a durability that few groups have enjoyed.

Three-part, closely spaced harmonies, multiple countermelodies, solos and every possibility in between have contributed to the trio's versatile sound. One hallmark of their style is the use of a solo voice or voices for the verses of a song, the three coming together in tight harmony for the chorus. From time to time, the three have made use of their respective solo voices in other musical contexts, with varying degrees of success, but it is their sound as a group that forms the basis of their lasting appeal.

LISTENING LIST
- "Blowin' in the Wind"
- "Day Is Done"
- "Five Hundred Miles"
- "I Dig Rock and Roll Music"
- "If I Had A Hammer"
- "Leaving on a Jet Plane"
- "Lemon Tree"
- "Puff the Magic Dragon"
- "This Land Is Your Land"
- "Where Have All the Flowers Gone?"

Peter, Paul and Mary's second album, Moving *(1963), remained on the charts for 99 weeks.*

THE KING'S SINGERS

As their name suggests, the King's Singers originated in England, a nation with a long and varied tradition of vocal music. The roots of the group were planted in 1965, when the 14 (all male) choral scholars at King's College, Cambridge decided to make a record of some of their "fun" repertoire. Six of the 14 later went on tour and were a great success. The name "King's Singers" was adopted in 1968, when the group made its London debut. Over the years, the King's Singers have performed with such diverse artists as Placido Domingo, the Boston Pops and Paul McCartney.

Both the personnel and the configuration of the King's Singers vary from time to time. In some seasons, for example, the group has been made up of a *countertenor* (a very high tenor), two tenors, two baritones, and a bass, while in other seasons one or more different male voice types may be substituted. (In 1968 and 1969, the group added a female voice to its ranks.) The group sings primarily a cappella music, covering the gamut from Bach to rock. The King's Singers have also commissioned specially written works and arrangements from a number of composers.

LISTENING LIST (ALBUMS)
Beatles Connection

Chanson d'Amour

Good Vibrations

Here's a Howdy Do: A Gilbert & Sullivan Festival

King's Singers Believe in Music

Little Christmas Music

Madrigal History Tour

On the Beautiful Blue Danube

This Is the King's Singers

A Tribute to the Comedian Harmonists

The King's Singers' 1993 album Good Vibrations *includes arrangements of songs made popular by the Beach Boys, Queen, U2 and other supergroups.*

PHOTO BY FRANK SCHULTZE/ZEITENSPIEGEL

SIMON AND GARFUNKEL

The duo of Simon and Garfunkel was one of the most successful folk-rock acts of the 1960s. They were known for their pure, high, choirboy-like harmonies, interesting guitar parts and well-crafted songs. Their "clean" sound was viewed by some as unhip during the psychedelic era, and Garfunkel's high tenor led some to label the duo as collegiate and sterile. Their vocal parts, however, were groundbreaking, combining sweet harmonies and the sounds of electric rock.

Paul Simon (born 1941) and Art Garfunkel (born 1941) met in grade school and debuted at a school assembly with an a cappella version of "Sh-Boom." Soon after, they were singing in a *doo-wop* (R&B- or rock-influenced harmony singing) group called the Sparks. Garfunkel's parents had two tape recorders, and the duo experimented with layering and recording their harmonies. Their professional recording history began in 1957, when they sang in the style of the Everly Brothers, using sweet, simple harmonies. After a few years, their careers seemed to be going nowhere, and they split up.

By the early 1960s the folk scene was growing, and in 1964, Simon and Garfunkel got back together and signed a contract with Columbia, resulting in their initially unsuccessful debut album. In 1965, producer Tom Wilson suggested augmenting their song "The Sounds of Silence" with electric guitar, bass and drums. The song reached number one on the charts. The duo went on to record five more albums, including a number of hits. Many of their songs used Latin rhythms and gospel influences that foreshadowed the sound of Simon's music in the 1980s and 1990s. Though they parted ways in the 1970s, Simon and Garfunkel have occasionally reunited for recordings and concerts.

LISTENING LIST
"The Boxer"
"Bridge over Troubled Water"
"El Condor Pasa"
"Homeward Bound"
"I Am a Rock"
"Mrs. Robinson"
"The Sounds of Silence"
"Scarborough Fair"

Simon and Garfunkel's 1981 reunion concert in New York's Central Park attracted half a million fans.

THE MANHATTAN TRANSFER

Since the early 1970s, the Manhattan Transfer has recorded and performed jazz, R&B and pop music in the style of Lambert, Hendricks and Ross. The group first became known for arrangements in which lyrics were added to previously recorded jazz instrumental pieces, a style that had been dormant since the mid-1960s. The Manhattan Transfer, made up of two male and two female voices, tried to "cross over" and make this style more commercially viable.

Although the Manhattan Transfer enjoyed success in the 1970s, it wasn't until 1981 that they scored their first top-ten hit with the 1965 girl-group classic "Boy from New York City." With commercial success came critical success. They became the first artists to win Grammy awards in pop and jazz categories in the same year, and their album *Vocalese* received 12 Grammy nominations.

In 1985 they began to move away from the something-for-everyone diversity of their earlier recordings and embarked on a series of recordings that featured a single concept or theme per album. Among these well-received recordings were albums devoted to Christmas music, Brazilian music, and even one based on the children's classic *Tubby the Tuba*. Though some personnel have changed over the course of the group's history, the Manhattan Transfer managed to retain a loyal following into the twenty-first century, as evidenced by their continued popularity as a live act and by recordings like *Spirit of St. Louis* (2000).

LISTENING LIST
- "Birdland"
- "Boy from New York City"
- "Java Jive"
- "A Nightingale Sang in Berkeley Square"
- "Operator"
- "That's Killer Joe"

The Manhattan Transfer *won their first Grammy for the 1979 album* Extensions.

DECADE: THE 1920s

In the aftermath of World War I, people were anxious to kick up their heels, and they did so with a vengeance. It wasn't by accident that the following decade came to be known as the Roaring '20s. The driving force of 1920s culture—aside from bathtub hooch—was jazz, and it was jazz that became the first truly American musical phenomenon to spread around the world. Though it was already a few decades old, the recording industry virtually exploded in the 1920s, and in response to the constant demand for novel sounds and new talent, vocal artists of every stripe emerged in droves to immortalize their voices in wax. Some became legends, some became one-hit wonders and some never quite made the big time, but the net result was a colorful, vibrant and still-vital musical legacy.

One of the most distinctive vocal styles to emerge in the 1920s was *crooning*, the smooth, suave vocal sound that made stars—even sex symbols—of Rudy Vallée, Gene Austin, and "Whispering" Jack Smith. On the opposite end of the spectrum, exuberant, vaudeville-trained singers like Al Jolson and Eddie Cantor electrified audiences with a super-charged, high-energy stage presence, which propelled both singers into movie careers. (Jolson, in fact, earned a place in history as the star of the very first "talkie," *The Jazz Singer*, in 1927.) 1920s audiences loved novelty in any form, and a number of singers parlayed rather distinctive vocal styles into legitimate success. Helium-voiced "boop-boop-a-doop" girl Helen Kane reached number two on the charts with "I Wanna Be Loved by You," but gained true immortality as the inspiration and model for animated star Betty Boop.

LISTENING LIST

Fred and Adele Astaire	"I'd Rather Charleston"
Gene Austin	"Ain't She Sweet?"
Eddie Cantor	"If You Knew Susie (Like I Know Susie)"
Al Jolson	"Toot, Toot, Tootsie"
Helen Kane	"I Wanna Be Loved by You"
Bessie Smith	"St. Louis Blues"
"Whispering" Jack Smith	"Miss Annabelle Lee"
Rudy Vallée	"My Time Is Your Time"

Bessie Smith, one of the greatest blues vocalists in history, electrified 1920s audiences with such recordings as "Down Hearted Blues" and "Jailhouse Blues."

DECADE: THE 1930s

Money was scarce in the Depression-stricken 1930s, so people did what they could to make their lives happy. Songs like "Life Is Just a Bowl of Cherries" and "Happy Days Are Here Again" were meant to uplift spirits. Still, the downbeat lyrics of songs like "Brother, Can You Spare a Dime?" more accurately reflected the times. People danced to the big band sounds of Benny Goodman, Duke Ellington, Tommy Dorsey and Guy Lombardo. Such bands were often fronted by a vocalist. Sometimes, two singers would sing together, almost speaking or acting the lines.

Broadway entered its golden age, resulting in many of the musicals that have come to be recognized as classics. Show tunes included creative use of harmonies, intervals and vocal techniques. Such vocal groups as the Boswell Sisters, the Andrews Sisters, the Mills Brothers and the Ink Spots showed off more traditional four-part harmonies.

In 1936, the U.S. Department of the Interior hired songwriter Woody Guthrie to travel throughout the American Northwest and perform folk songs. Guthrie's music helped set the tone for the folk scene in the following decades.

LISTENING LIST

Andrews Sisters	"Bei Mir Bist Du Schön"
Boswell Sisters	"Alexander's Ragtime Band"
Duke Ellington	"It Don't Mean a Thing If It Ain't Got That Swing"
Ink Spots	"If I Didn't Care"
Guy Lombardo	"Happy Days Are Here Again"
Teddy Wilson/Billie Holiday	"I Can't Give You Anything but Love"

PHOTO BY STEVE JOSTER • COURTESY OF STAR FILE PHOTO, INC.

Bing Crosby was one of the most popular entertainers of the twentieth century. Equally gifted as a singer and actor, he was a three-time Best Actor Oscar nominee. He took home the statuette for his performance in Going My Way *(1944), in which he performed his hit "Swingin' on a Star."*

DECADE: THE 1940s

World War II dominated the 1940s. Women took over jobs that had traditionally been associated with men, and society was changing. At the beginning of the decade, big bands still dominated popular music. Eventually, many of the singers who had worked with the bands went out on their own, and vocalists like Bing Crosby, Frank Sinatra, Dinah Shore, Kate Smith and Perry Como topped the charts. Big band singers like Billie Holiday and Ella Fitzgerald teamed up with other vocalists. Some vocal groups, such as the Pied Pipers, fronted a band or backed the lead singer.

Duos and vocal groups still had their place in the hit parade. Groups like the Three Flames, the Weavers and Three Suns made a name for themselves. The Mills Brothers created such a full sound with their voices that no one could believe they were accompanied only by a single guitar. The Ink Spots, one of the first black vocal groups to attain widespread popularity, helped pave the way for the doo-wop sound of the 1950s.

At the end of the decade, *bebop* (a harmonically and rhythmically complex jazz style) and R&B grew out of the big band era. Radios, jukeboxes and eventually televisions brought music of every style to the masses.

LISTENING LIST

Bing Crosby/Andrews Sisters	"Don't Fence Me In"
Ella Fitzgerald/Louis Jordan	"Baby It's Cold Outside"
Helen Forrest/Dick Haymes	"It Had to Be You"
Judy Garland/Gene Kelly	"For Me and My Gal"
Mills Brothers	"Paper Doll"
Pied Pipers	"Blues in the Night"
Jo Stafford/Gordon MacRae	"'A'—You're Adorable"

*During the 1940s, **Ella Fitzgerald** recorded a string of hits with the Ink Spots, Louis Jordan, the Delta Rhythm Boys and others.*

DECADE: THE 1950s

After World War II, American industry expanded, and people began to spend again, creating corporate expansion and jobs. The baby boom had begun. "Traditional" vocal groups like the Ames Brothers, the Four Aces and the McGuire Sisters were still popular.

As the 1950s continued, rock and roll was born. The smooth, tightly knit harmonies and vocal lines of "adult" singers were replaced by the loud, raucous sound of rock; the word "rock" even found its way into many song lyrics. Solo rock acts such as Elvis Presley often used a small chorus of voices to echo vocal lines. Harmony lines would occasionally be added, but instead of voices, electric instruments filled out the sound.

As radio, television and the recording industry grew, various styles of music now found an audience. As rock flourished, there was still an interest in four-part vocal groups and solo vocalists like Pat Boone. Folk music gained popularity with the emergence of such groups as the Kingston Trio.

LISTENING LIST

Chordettes	"Never on Sunday"
Everly Brothers	"Dream"
Five Satins	"In the Still of The Night"
Four Aces	"Three Coins in the Fountain"
Four Lads	"Istanbul (Not Constantinople)"
Bill Haley	"See You Later, Alligator"
Buddy Holly	"That'll Be the Day"
Kingston Trio	"Tom Dooley"
Lennon Sisters	"Sentimental Journey"
Platters	"The Great Pretender"
Elvis Presley	"Don't Be Cruel"

*The **Everly Brothers** scored their first chart hit with "Bye Bye Love," which reached number two in 1957.*

DECADE: THE 1960s

The 1960s saw a movement away from the conservative 1950s. Political and social changes affected values, lifestyles and music. Elvis Presley and other male vocalists like Neil Sedaka, Jerry Lee Lewis and Frankie Avalon still topped the charts. The Motown record label came on the scene with such vocal groups as Martha and the Vandellas, the Supremes and the Temptations. Vocal groups used traditional harmonies, now with a rock-oriented instrumental accompaniment. A folk music movement headed by the likes of Bob Dylan, Joan Baez and Peter, Paul and Mary proved to be highly influential. The folk sound was marked by acoustic guitars and songs with social or political messages.

Rock and roll was still going strong in the 1960s. The Beach Boys, Simon and Garfunkel and Crosby, Stills, Nash and Young sang a combination of folk and rock music. The strong melodies, rich voices and interesting arrangements of these groups are still considered some of the best ever. One of the greatest influences on American music in the 1960s was the "British Invasion" led by the Beatles. The Beatles' vocal styles changed with the times; in their earliest days, they sang traditional four-part arrangements, while, with the rise of the drug scene and *acid rock* (drug-influenced, guitar-heavy rock), their sound became less traditional and more amplified and improvisational.

LISTENING LIST

Beach Boys	"In My Room"
Beatles	"I Wanna Hold Your Hand"
Bee Gees	"Gotta Get a Message to You"
Chiffons	"One Fine Day"
Crosby, Stills, Nash and Young	"Helplessly Hoping"
Four Seasons	"Big Girls Don't Cry"
Highwaymen	"Michael Row the Boat Ashore"
Martha and the Vandellas	"Heat Wave"
Peter, Paul and Mary	"If I Had a Hammer"
Righteous Brothers	"You've Lost That Lovin' Feelin'"
Neil Sedaka	"Breaking Up Is Hard to Do"
Simon and Garfunkel	"Scarborough Fair"

*The **Beach Boys**' album* Pet Sounds *(1966) is widely regarded as one of the most influential rock albums ever recorded.*

DECADE: THE 1970s

The political and social chaos of the 1960s continued into the 1970s. The women's movement and the struggle for civil rights led to great social change. With the death of Elvis Presley and the breakup of the Beatles, rock and roll splintered into a number of distinct categories: classic rock, folk rock, soft rock, disco and *punk* (a fast, loud, energetic rock style).

The folk rock of groups like Simon and Garfunkel and Crosby, Stills, Nash and Young, which featured mainly acoustic instruments and tight vocal harmonies, was still popular. Such favorite soft-rock bands as the Bee Gees, ABBA, Seals and Crofts, and Hall and Oates featured a fuller, slightly more electric sound. The Eagles and Fleetwood Mac attained such great popularity that their harmonies are still imitated today. The Motown style continued to evolve in the music of bands like the Temptations, the Jackson 5, Earth, Wind and Fire, and the Commodores. Solo vocal acts like Elton John and Billy Joel also enjoyed success through the decade and beyond.

LISTENING LIST

ABBA	"Dancing Queen"
Bee Gees	"How Can You Mend a Broken Heart"
Eagles	"Hotel California"
Fleetwood Mac	"Landslide"
Jackson 5	"ABC"
KC and the Sunshine Band	"That's the Way I Like It"
Seals and Crofts	"Summer Breeze"
Tony Orlando and Dawn	"Knock Three Times"
Temptations	"Just My Imagination"

After pursuing solo careers with varying degrees of success, the **Jackson 5** reunited to record the album 2300 Jackson Street in 1989.

DECADE: THE 1980s

The 1980s, a time when people wanted and had it all, became known as the "Me" decade. The rise of the music video and MTV meant that the way artists looked was as important as the way they sounded. New pop and rock genres—punk, rap, heavy metal, hip-hop and ska—emerged and gained a wide audience, though none was especially known for its vocal harmonies.

Electronic music opened up new avenues for rock and roll. *Techno* (electronic music characterized by extremely fast, repetitive rhythms) and other synthesizer-based styles became popular. Harmonies were often created by layering tracks rather than by using multiple voices. In general, vocal harmonies became less prominent in the recording mix than they had previously been. In the late 1980s, the boy-band craze took shape, helping to revive a style of a cappella vocal harmony that had its roots in the Motown groups of the 1960s.

LISTENING LIST

Beach Boys	"Kokomo"
Commodores	"Lady (You Bring Me Up)"
Heart	"These Dreams"
Huey Lewis and the News	"If This Is It"
Kool and the Gang	"Celebration"
Manhattan Transfer	"Boy from New York City"
New Kids on the Block	"I'll Be Loving You"
Barbra Streisand/Donna Summer	"No More Tears"

*The **Commodores** were formed by six Tuskegee Institute students in 1967.*

DECADE: THE 1990s

The 1990s marked the beginning of a new electronic age. The CD became the recording medium of choice, while computers changed the way people communicated with the rise of e-mail, the Internet and the World Wide Web. Synthesized music enjoyed great popularity, as did *grunge* (a hybrid of punk and heavy metal) and techno music, none of which highlighted vocal harmonies. The rise of multicultural awareness in the 1990s resulted in a surge of popularity in Latino and other ethnic musics.

Country music attracted an all-new audience in the 1990s. The sound of bands like the Dixie Chicks was based on vocal (in this case, three-part) harmonies, while popular solo artists like Garth Brooks and Trisha Yearwood teamed up to sing duos.

LISTENING LIST

98°	"I Do Cherish You"
Ace of Base	"Don't Turn Around"
All 4 One	"I Swear/I Can Love You Like That"
Backstreet Boys	"Quit Playin' Games With My Heart
Boyz II Men	"In the Still of the Night"
Cranberries	"Linger"
Dixie Chicks	"Wide Open Spaces"
En Vogue	"Whatta Man"
Spice Girls	"Wannabe"
TLC	"Waterfalls"

*The **Dixie Chicks**' 1998 album* Wide Open Spaces *is the best-selling duo or group album in country music history.*

CONGRATULATIONS! YOU'RE A HARMONY SINGER!

By now, you have enough information to begin to sing harmony. You've come a long way. If you'd like to go further, you might want to consider voice lessons or even lessons on an instrument like piano or guitar. Any musical experience you can gain will be helpful to you when it comes to singing harmony.

As you continue to sing harmony, make sure that you're comfortable with your own voice. Sing a lot, and listen to recordings of yourself at every opportunity. Always warm up before you begin to sing. Make sure that the exercises and parts you sing are in a good range for your voice.

Once you are comfortable hearing your own voice, find a friend to sing two-part arrangements with you. Soon, you'll be secure enough to sing your part perfectly, even when more parts are added. After you're able to sing any written harmony line, it'll be time to move on to creating your own vocal harmonies. Practice writing out harmony parts and identifying the chords in a song. Next, sing along with recordings and experiment with creating harmonies spontaneously. Remember: Practice makes perfect.

SPEBSQSA is the "short" name for the Society for the Preservation and Encouragement of Barbershop Quartet Singing in America.

The eerie "monolith" music in 2001: A Space Odyssey is actually a work for 16 voices, Lux aeterna, by Hungarian composer György Ligeti.

The Andrews Sisters' hit "Boogie Woogie Bugle Boy" was introduced in the 1941 Abbott and Costello movie Buck Privates.

After the breakup of the pioneering jazz vocal group Lambert, Hendricks and Ross, singer Annie Ross branched out into film, including a turn as a villainess in Superman III (1983).

GLOSSARY OF MUSICAL TERMS

a cappella Vocal music without instrumental accompaniment

accidental A sign (usually ♯, ♭ or ♮) that changes the pitch of the note it precedes

accompaniment Music that supports the singers or instruments that have the main melody

alto (Short for **contralto**) The female voice with the lowest range

baritone A male voice with a range between that of the tenor and the bass

bass The male voice with the lowest range

beat The basic pulse in music

canon A musical work in which a melody is imitated for its entire length in one or more other parts

chord A group of three or more notes played at the same time

chromatic tone A tone that falls outside a particular scale

clef A sign at the beginning of a staff that indicates the pitch for each of the staff's lines and spaces

contralto See **alto**

counterpoint The simultaneous combination of two or more independent melodies

diaphragm A dome-shaped muscle that divides the chest cavity from the abdominal cavity

falsetto The high "head voice" above a singer's normal range (usually applied to male singers)

flat A sign (♭) that lowers a pitch by a half step

harmony The result of two pitches sounded simultaneously

hymn A song of praise or adoration.

improvise To make up music as it is being played or sung, as opposed to using music that has already been composed

interval The distance between two pitches

inversion A chord in which a tone other than the root is in the bass

key The tonal center of a piece of music

key signature The sharps or flats just to the right of a clef that indicate the key of a piece of music

larynx Voice box; the apparatus that contains the vocal cords

lungs Membranous sacs located in the chest that produce breath

major scale The arrangement of eight pitches into the following pattern of whole steps and half steps: W W H W W W H

measure The musical space contained between two bar lines

melody A tune or theme made up of a distinctive sequence of notes

natural sign A sign (♮) that cancels a sharp or flat

nonharmonic tone A tone that is not part of a chord

note A tone that has specific pitch and duration

octave The shortest distance between two notes of the same name

ostinato A short, repeated figure often used as a bass line

palate The roof of the mouth

part In music for multiple voices, a line for a single voice that is one component of the overall texture

pickup An incomplete measure at the beginning of a musical work that begins after the downbeat

pitch The exact degree of a note's highness or lowness

polyphony Music that makes use of more than one independent part

range The entire compass, from low to high, of the pitches that can be produced by a singer

register A specific portion of a singer's entire range

resonance The enrichment of vocal sound within the mouth, nasal cavity and sinuses

rest In musical notation, a symbol indicating silence

rhythm The pattern of short and long sounds and silences in music

round A song in which voices sing the same melody, each entering in turn at a different point

scale An arrangement of pitches according to a specific pattern of whole steps and half steps

sharp A sign (♯) that raises a pitch by a half step

solo A musical passage or complete work for a single voice or instrument

soprano The female voice with the highest range

staff The set of five lines and four spaces on which music is notated

tempo The speed at which a piece of music is played or sung

tenor The male voice with the highest range. A tenor with a very high range is called a **countertenor**.

theme A melody or a short sequence of notes on which a piece of music is based

tie In musical notation, a curved line that joins the values of two notes of the same pitch

time signature A pair of numbers at the beginning of a piece of music that indicates the number of beats in a measure and the note value of those beats

timbre The unique identifying quality of a sound

triad A chord consisting of three tones, named, from the bottom up, the root, 3rd and 5th

triplets A group of three equal notes played in the time of two of the same value

unison The singing or playing of two voices at the same pitch

vocal cords Muscular folds in the larynx that vibrate when air passes through them, producing vocal sound

voice box See **larynx**